EXPOSING PROPHETIC WITCHCRAFT

Destiny Image Books by Jennifer LeClaire

EXPOSING PROPHETIC WITCHCRAFT

IDENTIFYING TELL-TALE SIGNS OF SATAN'S COUNTERFEIT MESSENGERS

JENNIFER LECLAIRE

DESTINY IMAGE® PUBLISHERS, INC.
P.O. Box 310, Shippensburg, PA 17257-0310
"Promoting Inspired Lives."

This book and all other Destiny Image and Destiny Image Fiction books are available at Christian bookstores and distributors worldwide.

For more information on foreign distributors, call 717-532-3040.

Reach us on the Internet: www.destinyimage.com.

ISBN 13 TP: 978-0-7684-6278-4

ISBN 13 eBook: 978-0-7684-6279-1

ISBN 13 HC: 978-0-7684-6281-4

ISBN 13 LP: 978-0-7684-6280-7

For Worldwide Distribution, Printed in the U.S.A.

1 2 3 4 5 6 7 8 / 26 25 24 23 22

DEDICATION

This book is dedicated to Christian International, a movement of prophetic equippers and prophets who are dedicated to seeing the true prophetic movement go forward. I have benefited personally and in ministry from the integrity of Bishop Bill Hamon, as well his revelations on spiritual warfare. Bishop Hamon has always been my hero in the prophetic, and I can't thank him enough for his service to the Body of Christ.

ACKNOWLEDGEMENTS

I'm so grateful for my family of intercessors, Awakening Prayer Hubs and Awakening House of Prayer, who stand with me against the wiles of the enemy in the nations of the earth. I could not do what I do without your intercession. I'm thankful to the Destiny Image team, led by Larry Sparks, who has a keen sense of what the Lord wants to say to the church in this hour. His heart for revival, passion for God, and stance against the works of darkness are benefiting the Bride.

CONTENTS

A TROUBLING DREAM ABOUT JEZEBEL'S
WITCHCRAFT

had a profound dream about Jezebel. In the dream, Jezebel organized a plot to destroy my prophetic voice. I didn't recognize it at first. This spirit was operating through a person and was so extremely subtle that the spirit was at first unrecognizable.

This person, who was a symbol of Jezebel, was trying to woo me into a marriage covenant. Jezebel gave me all sorts of what sounded to the natural mind "strategic reasons" to engage in this covenant.

At first, I rejected all the proposals, discerning some perversion under the surface. I couldn't put my finger on it. Jezebel in disguise persisted with all the reasoning and wisdom, even presenting contracts and rings. After giving ear to Jezebel for some time, I started to fall under this principality's spell. I was bewitched.

How did it happen? While at first I was unwilling to consider a contract, Jezebel kept nagging me the way Delilah nagged Samson, and I found myself willing to give an ear to the proposals. I found myself beginning to agree with what Jezebel was saying. Jezebel was pleased that I was starting to see things its way.

Jezebel in disguise then wanted to sleep in my bed. That's when I snapped out of the bewitchment and offered a firm, "No!" (The devil always overplays his hand.) But Jezebel did not take no for answer. I said, "Jezebel, my bed is not big enough for the both of us." In other words, I would not get in bed with Jezebel!

Jezebel continued reasoning and suggested buying a bigger bed. I persisted in saying no. I rejected Jezebel. I saw the assignment for what it was and aggressively stood against it. Again, I refused to get into bed with Jezebel.

What is going on? This dream was not about me alone. In this dream, I represented the prophetic movement. Remember, Jezebel is a spirit of seduction and operates in false prophecy. I believe Jezebel in disguise has bewitched too many in the prophetic movement. The fact that I gave ear to Jezebel at all in this dream shows you just how subtle the spirit can be.

The Bible speaks clearly of Jezebel and her witchcrafts (see 2 Kings 9:22). Some prophets are agreeing with Jezebel and persecuting other prophets, while other prophets are eating at Jezebel's table and she is sleeping in their bed. Still other prophets are staying pure, like Elijah and the 7,000 others who would not bow a knee to idolatry.

I wrote about these types of issues extensively in my book *Discerning Prophetic Witchcraft*. In the book, I wrote about a 20-year-old prophetic word the Lord gave me about a prophetic showdown. I believe that showdown, or at least the first phase of it, is upon us. With so much division in the prophetic movement, it's easier for spirits like Jezebel to come in unawares.

It's time for prophets to check their hearts for compromise with Jezebel. It's time for prophets to guard their hearts from Jezebelic influences. When you suggest that anyone who does not believe your prophecy is bowing to Jezebel, it's possible that you are the one bowing to this controlling, seductive spirit.

Some prophets have made covenants with Jezebel. Some prophets have made covenants with mammon. Some prophets have made covenants with spirits other than the Holy Spirit. This can happen to anyone who gives ear to seductive voices for too long. And remember, Jezebel's voice is subtle. Don't give your ear to Jezebel long enough to fall under its spell. Rather, only listen long enough to discern the spirit's operations and then flee immorality.

If you have been agreeing with Jezebel, eating at Jezebel's table, or in bed with Jezebel, now is the time to repent and take your true voice back. God can restore your voice. God wants to restore your voice. Even Elijah gave in to the voice of Jezebel and ran and hid in a cave. If you've been listening to the wrong voice, you can change frequencies. God can deliver you from compromise and restore your office.

And, I should add, you don't have to be a prophet to fall under Jezebel's spell. She attacks anyone with a prophetic voice and wants to hijack your soul, making you into a prophetic manipulator who releases prophetic witchcraft in the Kingdom of God.

CHAPTER 1

EXPOSING THE WOLVES IN SHEEP'S
CLOTHING

F raudsters love to target the elderly. You may have heard the story—it went absolutely viral in many nations—about a retired woman who was stricken with illness. She was waiting for her granddaughter to bring her a meal, so when she heard a "knock, knock" she gladly opened the door. Only it wasn't her granddaughter at all. It was a wolf in disguise. Before grandma could act, the wolf devoured her.

That story, of course, is *Little Red Riding Hood* and it has parallels to wolves in sheep's clothing—also known as false prophets—today. If you recall the fictional classic, the wolf devoured grandma in a single mouthful and waited for Little Red Riding Hood, whom he had met on the path along the way, to show up so he could devour her too. When the young girl showed up, the wolf was dressed in grandma's clothing and was imitating grandma's voice.

"What a deep voice you have," said the little girl in surprise.

"The better to greet you with," said the wolf.

"Goodness, what big eyes you have."

"The better to see you with."

"And what big hands you have!" exclaimed Little Red Riding Hood, stepping over to the bed.

"The better to hug you with," said the wolf.

"What a big mouth you have," the little girl murmured in a weak voice.

"The better to eat you with!" growled the wolf, and jumping out of bed, he swallowed her up too. Then, with a fat, full tummy, he fell fast asleep.

Thankfully, a hunter who had been on the wolf's trail found the scheming wolf sleeping, shot him, cut his belly open, and delivered the grandma and the child safely. When Little Red Riding Hood finally returned home to her worried mother, she shared a valuable lesson she learned: "We must always keep on the path and never stop. That way, we come to no harm!" Little Red Riding Hood's lesson is strategic for the church. God has called us to walk on the narrow path and not stray from it. There's danger on the broad path.

Indeed, in the last moments of the Sermon on the Mount, Jesus shared these sobering words:

> *Enter by the narrow gate; for wide is the gate and broad is the way that leads to destruction, and there are many who go in by it. Because narrow is the gate and difficult is the way which leads to life, and there are few who find it* (Matthew 7:13-14).

Little Red Riding Hood was warned not to stray from the narrow path that led to grandma's house. But she was distracted, first by bright red strawberries, then by beautiful butterflies, then by blooming flowers she joyfully picked for grandma. When she disregarded her mother's wise instruction, she got in trouble. She met the wolf, who conned her out of information about old granny. The wolf ran to granny's house to devour the unsuspecting elderly woman. He was essentially a wolf in sheep's clothing.

Although Christ's words about the narrow and broad gates speak about the path to salvation, it's clearly also the path of holiness. It's the path Christ calls us to walk. It's a path He walks with us. When we stray from His leadership down the broad path, we open ourselves up to attack—to destruction. Put another way, we open ourselves up to the wolf—the enemy who comes to steal, kill, and destroy (see John 10:10). And I believe some of those wolves are in sheep's clothing. Some of those wolves are operating in prophetic witchcraft.

It's no coincidence that right after Jesus spoke of the narrow gate in Matthew 7:14, He speaks of these wolves. Matthew 7:15-16 reads, "Beware of false prophets, who come to you in sheep's clothing, but inwardly they are ravenous wolves. You will know them by their fruits." When we stay on the narrow path, we won't seek out prophetic words because we'll hear the still small voice of the One who is leading us and guiding us. When we stay on the narrow path, we won't open ourselves up to the dangers from the Big Bad Wolf dressed like grandma setting out to deceive and devour us with prophetic witchcraft.

WHAT IS PROPHETIC WITCHCRAFT?

My first book on this topic, *Discerning Prophetic Witchcraft*, went in-depth into discerning this practice. In case you haven't read that book (and you should), it's helpful to understand what prophetic witchcraft and false prophets are before moving ahead.

A false prophet is not one who misses it or one who makes poor judgment calls in ministry operations as they learn and grow. No, a false prophet, in the simplest terms, is one who sets out to deceive. The motive is to gain something to consume upon their own lusts outside the will of God, whether that's money, fame, or some other reward. They don't seek God for what they need; rather, they manipulate their way into what they want.

Maybe you have never heard false prophetic utterance firsthand or witnessed the operation of a false seer—or maybe you just haven't discerned these false functions yet. Let me assure you, as one who has walked on the front lines of the prophetic movement for decades, false prophets and false seers are emerging rapidly with manipulative cunning. False prophets appear to the undiscerning eye as genuine, but they are seeking to devour. They seem sincere, but they are sincerely wrong in motive. It's important to exercise discernment, to examine the fruit rather than being enamored with a spiritual gift, charisma, or a large following.

But false prophets aren't the only ones who operate in prophetic witchcraft. Prophetic witchcraft is false prophecy, but it's the source of the prophecy that is concerning. While prophecy speaks the mind, will, and heart of God for a person, situation, or nation, prophetic witchcraft can oppose the will of God—or at least lead you into a different direction. Prophetic witchcraft taps into a spirit other than the Holy Spirit, who is the spirit of prophecy. Since the spirit of prophecy is the testimony of Jesus (see Rev. 19:10), prophetic witchcraft can't be the testimony of Jesus—or what Jesus is saying.

As the head of the church and our Savior, we want to hear the Holy Spirit report what Jesus is saying. Prophetic witchcraft could be what the prophet (or prophetic person) is saying in order to flatter, manipulate, or control you into giving your time, money, or loyalty to the prophesier. Prophetic witchcraft can also come from a spirit of divination, essentially a message straight from the enemy's camp. The message may sound like God, but that doesn't mean God said it.

What's so tricky for many people is prophetic witchcraft can be true—false prophetic people can speak accurate words—but that doesn't mean the information comes from God. Familiar spirits and other demons set out to deceive, and sometimes they set the bait for a hungry believer with an ounce of truth before selling them a pound of lies. Remember the girl from Thyatira who followed Paul and Silas around proclaiming they were men of God proclaiming the way to salvation? The Acts 16 incident is recorded so we would know that a spirit can operate through a person to share truth.

MY RUN-IN WITH A BONA FIDE WOLF

Soon after I wrote the book *Discerning Prophetic Witchcraft*, I caught a bona fide false prophet—we'll call him Derek—in action in my ministry. I met this person in another nation while on a ministry trip and found out we had some common acquaintances. This false prophet pursued me, served the ministry, and at first seemed like a blessing, but within about a month I discerned something was off. I didn't want to believe it because others I knew seemed to endorse him, and I had no proof. So I waited to see the fruits. Remember, Jesus said you will know false prophets by their fruits—and fruits take some time to grow.

I started to keep Derek at a distance. But because people in my church had seen him commenting on my social media posts—and I even invited him into one of my videos at one point before I discerned the motives—they started following him too. I had no idea he had adopted some of my young adults as spiritual sons and daughters and had them working in his ministry. I sort of wondered why they were dropping balls in the church but never had any idea he had convinced a small army of my volunteers to abandon their posts at Awakening House of Prayer to serve his ministry.

As I further distanced myself from Derek, he kept trying to reconnect. Finally, one day I saw him promoting a product and he told me one of my staff had edited it and translated it for him. I had no idea. I was waiting for this same volunteer to translate books for payment, but his was done first. Something hit my spirit wrong, but I didn't know what.

When I asked our volunteer—we'll call her Chelsea—how she ended up working on his project for free when my paid project was yet unfinished, we found out the ugly truth. She told us Derek prophesied—or should I say prophe-lied to her. He used prophetic witchcraft to convince her she was supposed to translate his books. She thought I knew and had blessed it. Derek also prophesied to her husband, her son, and her daughter and shared grand visions about missions trips to Chelsea's nation to bring medical supplies in droves. All false promises.

As it turns out, Derek was also prophesying to many others in my church, using prophetic witchcraft to draw them to himself. Finally, people in other nations started coming to me telling me what trouble he had caused in their ministries. The false prophet was exposed, but some of my church members were lost. But it was nothing compared to what we later found out he did in other churches. He was convincing married women that their husbands weren't doing enough to help his churches. Some of these women actually filed for divorce from their husbands to follow the wolf. That's extreme prophetic witchcraft.

That's when I saw how the wolf in sheep's clothing operates on a practical level, using prophetic witchcraft to seduce, flatter, deceive, and direct sheep like puppets on a string. These precious people who fall under the wolf's deception believe they are fulfilling the will of God—supporting the work of God financially or advancing the work of God with their labor of love. Little do they know they are sowing into a field that will be devoured by worms. They won't see a return on the seed they donated into the false prophet's ministry. And their works, because they are not motivated by love, will yield no eternal rewards in heaven.

Derek's actions made me angry—a righteous indignation. How dare the wolf dress up like a sheep and deceive generous, God-fearing, good-hearted people in my church and many other churches in several other nations! I know Jesus sends us out as lambs in the midst of wolves (see Luke 10:3), and we have to grow in discernment. We have to be wise as serpents and innocent as doves (see Matt. 10:16). Beyond Jesus, Paul the apostle warned us fierce wolves would come to attack us (see Acts 20:29).

That means discerning prophetic witchcraft is not enough. I have been walking in prophetic ministry for decades and the wolf was operating under my nose. Yes, I discerned something was off and I didn't let him into my soul, but he got into the heads and pocketbooks of some of the people under my care. So it's not enough that we discern prophetic witchcraft and the wolves in sheep's clothing who release it; we must expose prophetic witchcraft. That's what this book sets out to do in a biblical way. In Ephesians 5:6-13, Paul warned:

> *Let no one deceive you with empty words, for because of these things the wrath of God comes upon the sons of disobedience. Therefore do not be partakers with them. For you were once darkness, but now you are light in the Lord. Walk as children of light (for the fruit of the Spirit is in all goodness, righteousness, and truth), finding out what is acceptable to the Lord. And have no fellowship with the unfruitful works of darkness,*

but rather expose them. For it is shameful even to speak of those things which are done by them in secret. But all things that are exposed are made manifest by the light, for whatever makes manifest is light.

Paul said expose them. The Amplified Bible, Classic Edition of this verse puts it this way, "Take no part in and have no fellowship with the fruitless deeds and enterprises of darkness, but instead [let your lives be so in contrast as to] expose and reprove and convict them." And *The Message* boldly encourages:

Don't waste your time on useless work, mere busywork, the barren pursuits of darkness. Expose these things for the sham they are. It's a scandal when people waste their lives on things they must do in the darkness where no one will see. Rip the cover off those frauds and see how attractive they look in the light of Christ.

Let's rip the cover off. Let's expose prophetic witchcraft. Read this open letter to wolves in sheep's clothing and come into agreement that you see them. Pray God will expose them to you so you don't fall into their trap. I can't list every wolf in sheep's clothing as I do not know every person on the face of the earth. But I wrote this open letter to expose their operations to you and hopefully to some of the wolves who can't see what they are doing. I pray the wolves will recognize themselves in these words and turn from their wicked ways.

AN OPEN LETTER TO WOLVES IN SHEEP'S CLOTHING

Dear Wolves in Sheep's Clothing,

A growing number of people in the Body of Christ see you. The Holy Spirit is opening our eyes to your prophetic witchcraft and the motive behind it.

We have our eyes on you and we won't fall for your slick brand of deception anymore. You may have fooled us time and time again, but you will not fool us one more time.

Jesus not only warned us that you are ferocious wolves in disguise, He also warned us of your tactics. We know that you don't enter the sheepfold by the door. You aren't welcomed in, so you find some other way to steal, kill, and destroy (see John 10:10). You use manipulation and flattery. You use the hurts, wounds, desires, insecurities, and other soulish issues against us. You use our spiritual hunger and even our lack of discipline against us.

Jesus put it this way in John 10:1: "Most assuredly, I say to you, he who does not enter the sheepfold by the door, but climbs up some other way, the same is a thief and a robber."

I like how The Passion Translation says it: "Listen to this eternal truth: The person who sneaks over the wall to enter into the sheep pen, rather than coming through the gate, reveals himself as a thief coming to steal." If that's not clear enough, consider *The Message* rendition: "Let me set this before you as plainly as I can. If a person climbs over or through the fence of a sheep pen instead of going through the gate, you know he's up to no good—a sheep rustler!"

Wolves in Sheep's Clothing, you are exposed. As they say in Nicaragua, "An enemy exposed is an enemy defeated." You couldn't build your own ministry, so you had to seduce personnel from successful ministry leaders—but you will fail anyway. You couldn't build your own platform, so you had to weasel your way onto someone else's and prophesy to their followers until they followed you. You couldn't write your own book, so you had to plagiarize from another author's. You couldn't get a pure word from the Lord, so you had to recycle someone else's. I see you.

Wolves in Sheep's Clothing, you are exposed. You aren't willing to pay the price for the anointing, so you operate in hype. You aren't willing to sacrifice the time in prayer it takes to receive prophetic revelation, so you fake it and you think you made it—but you will soon fall headlong into the snare you set for your victims. You didn't study to show yourself approved, so you twist the Word for your own purposes. I see you.

Wolves in Sheep's Clothing, Jesus has sent us out in your midst and we are wise as serpents and harmless as doves (see Matt. 10:16). We are shrewd to your sinister sabotage. We are cautious and discerning to your ravenous ways. We are crafty against your wily witchcraft. We are prudent against your false prophetic power. Because we see you.

Wolves in Sheep's Clothing, your days are numbered. Although you may still be fooling some, you aren't fooling me and I'm raising up an army of uncompromising believers who will not violate the Bible to make a greenback. I'm raising up an army of discerning saints who will not sow greenbacks into your false prophetic ministry. I'm vowing to equip the Bride so she doesn't get in bed with a wolf. I see you.

Wolves in Sheep's Clothing, repent now. Because if you don't you'll soon hear Jesus saying these words:

> Not everyone who says to Me, "Lord, Lord," shall enter the kingdom of heaven, but he who does the will of My Father in heaven. Many will say to Me in that day, "Lord, Lord, have we not prophesied in Your name, cast out demons in Your name, and done many wonders in Your name?" And then I will declare to them, "I never knew you; depart from Me, you who practice lawlessness!" (Matthew 7:21-24)

Wolves in Sheep's Clothing, I see you. We see you. Most importantly, God sees you. You aren't getting away with it. There's a price to pay for deceiving God's people. Wolves in Sheep's Clothing, I'm praying for you. There's a better way. There's always time to repent. God is giving you that space to repent. Please, take it.

LESSONS FROM A WISE PIG

As we end this chapter, I want to point you to a familiar story of another wolf—the wolf in *The Three Little Pigs*. Don't skim over this, even if you've heard it before, and if you've never heard it, pay close attention because you'll find godly wisdom in the tale.

The story begins with three little pigs who left home to see the world. As the story goes, they had a blast and made a lot of friends, but when summer ended they realized they needed to make homes for themselves. They strategized among themselves, and each had a different idea of the ideal dwelling. The story reads:

The laziest little pig said he'd build a straw hut. "It will only take a day," he said. The others disagreed. "It's too fragile," they said disapprovingly, but he refused to listen. Not quite so lazy, the second little pig went in search of planks of seasoned wood. "Clunk! Clunk! Clunk!" It took him two days to nail them together. But the third little pig did not like the wooden house. "That's not the way to build a house!" he said. "It takes time, patience, and hard work to build a house that is strong enough to stand up to wind, rain, and snow, and most of all protect us from the wolf!"

Notice there were three little pigs, but only one built his future life with the wolf in mind. The wise little pig worked hard to build his house while his brothers were out having fun. He declared, "I shall not be foolish like you! For he who laughs last, laughs longest!" About that time, as the story goes, the wise little pig found wolf tracks. Soon enough the wolf manifested in their midst.

The lazy pig was in his straw hut when the wolf scowled fiercely, "Come out!" ordered the wolf, his mouth watering. "I want to speak to you!"

"I'd rather stay where I am!" replied the little pig in a tiny voice.

"I'll make you come out!" growled the wolf angrily, and puffing out his chest, he took a very deep breath. Then he blew with all his might, right onto the house. And all the straw the silly pig had heaped against some thin poles fell down in the great blast. Excited by his own cleverness, the wolf did not notice that the little pig had slithered out from underneath the heap of straw, and was dashing toward his brother's wooden house. When he realized that the little pig was escaping, the wolf grew wild with rage.

"Come back!" he roared, trying to catch the pig as he ran into the wooden house. The other little pig greeted his brother, shaking like a leaf.

"I hope this house won't fall down! Let's lean against the door so he can't break in!"

Outside, the wolf could hear the little pigs' words. Starving as he was, at the idea of a two-course meal, he rained blows on the door.

"Open up! Open up! I only want to speak to you!"

You know what happens next. The wolf huffed and puffed and blew the wooden house down. The wise little pig was watching and opened the door for his brothers just in the nick of time. The wolf huffed and puffed three times and could now blow the house down. Finally, the wolf wore himself out. At the end of the story, we find the other two little pigs working hard to build a brick house that the next wolf who came through could not blow down.

CHRIST WARNED ABOUT THE BIG BAD WOLVES

This is more than a cute story. This is a parallel to Jesus' words at the end of the Sermon on the Mount. Jesus taught us how to build our lives in the Sermon on the Mount. He taught us what we have come to call the Beatitudes, admonished us to be salt and light, explained how murder begins in the heart, warned us about judging, taught us the Lord's Prayer, fasting, giving, and much more.

In what is often called the Constitution of the Kingdom, Matthew chapters 5, 6, and 7 also warn us about false prophets. I wrote extensively about signs of false prophets in the first book in this trilogy, *Discerning Prophetic Witchcraft*, so we won't recount them here. But Christ gave a lengthy warning about those who operate in His name falsely in Matthew 7:15-23:

> *Beware of false prophets, who come to you in sheep's clothing, but inwardly they are ravenous wolves. You will know them by their fruits. Do men gather grapes from thornbushes or figs from thistles? Even so, every good tree bears good fruit, but a bad tree bears bad fruit. A good tree cannot bear bad fruit, nor can a bad tree bear good fruit. Every tree that does not bear good fruit is cut down and thrown into the fire. Therefore by their fruits you will know them.*
>
> *Not everyone who says to Me, "Lord, Lord," shall enter the kingdom of heaven, but he who does the will of My Father in*

*heaven. Many will say to Me in that day, "Lord, Lord, have
we not prophesied in Your name, cast out demons in Your
name, and done many wonders in Your name?" And then I
will declare to them, "I never knew you; depart from Me, you
who practice lawlessness!"*

Matthew 7:15-23 offer some heavy words. And it's no coincidence
that the verses immediately after offer a lesson that, in many ways, is
similar to *The Three Little Pigs*. In Matthew 7:24-27, we see Jesus talking
about both wise and foolish people who build their house and how they
build it. Listen in to these ageless words:

*Therefore whoever hears these sayings of Mine, and does them,
I will liken him to a wise man who built his house on the rock:
and the rain descended, the floods came, and the winds blew
and beat on that house; and it did not fall, for it was founded
on the rock. But everyone who hears these sayings of Mine,
and does not do them, will be like a foolish man who built his
house on the sand: and the rain descended, the floods came,
and the winds blew and beat on that house; and it fell. And
great was its fall.*

When we build our lives on prophetic witchcraft—when we build
our lives on the false promises that immature, presumptuous, or false
prophetic people speak into our lives—we are setting ourselves up for a
fall. God has no obligation to sustain what He didn't build. As a matter
of fact, Psalm 127:1 tells us plainly, "Unless the Lord builds the house,
they labor in vain who build it."

A keen strategy of the enemy to steal, kill, and destroy is to get you
to believe a lie—in this case a false prophecy—and set out to build your

life on it. You may indeed build something, but the same enemy who deceived you will soon come huffing and puffing to blow your house down so he can feast on your failure and cause you to despise prophecy. Peter warned us the enemy comes like a roaring lion seeking someone to devour (see 1 Pet. 5:8). That is true, but sometimes the enemy comes as a wolf in sheep's clothing seeking to devour. And that should offend you.

I'm reminded of one of Aesop's fables: "A wolf was chasing a lamb, which took refuge in a temple. The wolf urged it to come out of the precincts, and said, 'If you don't, the priest is sure to catch you and offer you up in sacrifice on the altar.' To which the lamb replied, 'Thanks, I think I'll stay where I am. I'd rather be sacrificed any day than be eaten up by a wolf.'" I pray this book helps you see the wolves.

CHAPTER 2

PROPHETIC WITCHCRAFT SHOULD
OFFEND YOU

Offense is a key weapon of the enemy and most of us have plenty of opportunities to be offended in the church world (let alone at home or in the workplace). Some people are offended by women in ministry. Others are offended because the pastor doesn't say "hello" to them when they walk through the sanctuary. Still others are offended because they didn't get on the worship team or because someone sat in their seat at church.

Unfortunately, many people are offended every day over mere misunderstandings or unrealistic expectations and leave their church home in a huff looking for a "more loving church." Indeed, many blood-bought, prophesying, church-going, Bible-believing, charismatic, tongue-talking believers leave churches offended every day without ever expressing what upset them so it can be clarified and rectified. I believe offense is opening the door up to deception. When we leave a safe place offended, we are open prey for wolves in sheep's clothing.

Many years ago, I saw a truth in Scripture that has haunted me. When I say haunted me, I mean it has stuck in my mind like Hubba Bubba gum in red, curly hair. I have never forgotten the Scriptures in which Jesus makes a clear connection—and demonstrates the clear progression—toward an offended heart and the false prophet brand of deception. Indeed, these words of Jesus are telling, and I pray they stick to you like Elmer's glue.

We find these sobering words of warning in Christ's discourse about the end times. Before I share the words, let me paint a picture of the scene. Jesus had just predicted the destruction of the temple. He sat down on the Mount of Olives and His disciples came to Him privately asking when the temple would fall and for a heads-up on the signs of His coming and the end of the age (see Matt. 24:1-3). That's when Jesus laid a heavy message on them that draws undeniable and direct parallels between offense and prophetic witchcraft.

DON'T LET ANYONE DECEIVE YOU

Here's what Jesus, the Faithful Witness, said in Matthew 24:4-14:

Take heed that no one deceives you. For many will come in My name, saying, "I am the Christ," and will deceive many. And you will hear of wars and rumors of wars. See that you are not troubled; for all these things must come to pass, but the end is not yet. For nation will rise against nation, and kingdom against kingdom. And there will be famines, pestilences, and earthquakes in various places. All these are the beginning of sorrows.

Then they will deliver you up to tribulation and kill you, and you will be hated by all nations for My name's sake. And then many will be offended, will betray one another, and will hate one another. Then many false prophets will rise up and deceive many. And because lawlessness will abound, the love of many will grow cold. But he who endures to the end shall be saved. And this gospel of the kingdom will be preached in all the world as a witness to all the nations, and then the end will come.

In one of His final messages on earth, Jesus urgently warned us not to be deceived. In fact, you can't read a single book in the New Testament that does not warn of deception or false prophets, false teachers, or false apostles. But take note of verses 10 and 11: "And then many will be offended, will betray one another, and will hate one another. Then many false prophets will rise up and deceive many."

Can you see it? An offended heart is prey for false prophets and their weaponized prophetic witchcraft. An offended heart dilutes our discernment. An offended heart can't see the truth. That's why we need to cultivate a fiery hot love walk. Love is not easily offended (see 1 Cor. 13:5). In fact, love covers all offenses (see Prov. 10:12).

The Passion Translation puts Matthew 24:10-11 this way: "And many lying prophets will arise, deceiving multitudes and leading them away from the path of truth." Jesus wasn't warning a relative handful of people about the danger of prophetic witchcraft. He was warning that masses would be deceived. That means we must become un-offendable, or at least only take offense to what offends God.

PROPHETIC WITCHCRAFT IS OFFENSIVE TO GOD

God can be offended, but it's not the same type of offense we take on when our expectations are not met or when someone makes a rude comment. Sin, for example, offends God because He is holy. Some of what God hates He calls abominations:

> *These six things the Lord hates, yes, seven are an abomination to Him: a proud look, a lying tongue, hands that shed innocent blood, a heart that devises wicked plans, feet that are swift in running to evil, a false witness who speaks lies, and one who sows discord among brethren* (Proverbs 6:16-19).

Jesus, the Prophet, is called the Faithful Witness (see Rev. 1:5). False prophets are among the false witnesses who speak lies that God hates. As servants of the Lord, we are called to love what God loves and hate what God hates. Prophetic witchcraft should be offensive to you because it's offensive to the Lord. Prophetic witchcraft mimics the true voice of God in a counterfeit operation to lead people astray. God doesn't like anyone putting words in His mouth.

Paul warned us not to grieve the Holy Spirit. The Greek word for *grieve* in that verse is *lupeo*, and one of the definitions is "offend," according to *The KJV New Testament Greek Lexicon*.

Prophetic witchcraft grieves, or offends, the Holy Spirit, who is the spirit of prophecy. The prophet Isaiah offers insight on what we reap when we embrace what God hates: "Woe (judgment is coming) to those who call evil good, and good evil; who substitute darkness for light and light for darkness; who substitute bitter for sweet and sweet for bitter!" (Isa. 5:20 AMP).

Hananiah was releasing prophetic witchcraft in Israel in Jeremiah's day. He was prophesying in the house of God to the priests and the people. His prophecy?

> *"I have broken the yoke of the king of Babylon. Within two full years I will bring back to this place all the vessels of the Lord's house, that Nebuchadnezzar king of Babylon took away from this place and carried to Babylon. And I will bring back to this place Jeconiah the son of Jehoiakim, king of Judah, with all the captives of Judah who went to Babylon," says the Lord, "for I will break the yoke of the king of Babylon"* (Jeremiah 28:2-4).

This was contrary to what many others prophesied and was surely a popular prophecy because, after all, who wants to hear a weeping prophet predicting judgment and long-term captivity? So what did Jeremiah do? He agreed that he would like to see Hananiah's words come to pass, but he prophesied the opposite of Hananiah's word. In other words, he confronted the false prophecy head-on. Hananiah kept contending for his false prophecy, even doing a prophetic act to convince the people of his words.

> *Then Hananiah the prophet took the yoke off the prophet Jeremiah's neck and broke it. And Hananiah spoke in the presence of all the people, saying, "Thus says the Lord: 'Even so I will break the yoke of Nebuchadnezzar king of Babylon from the neck of all nations within the space of two full years'"* (Jeremiah 28:10-11).

Jeremiah wasn't going to sit there and argue with a false prophet. He left and sought the Lord, who told him exactly how to deal with the false prophet's prophetic witchcraft. Beware, what you are about to read is shocking.

> *Then the prophet Jeremiah said to Hananiah the prophet, "Hear now, Hananiah, the Lord has not sent you, but you*

make this people trust in a lie. Therefore thus says the Lord: 'Behold, I will cast you from the face of the earth. This year you shall die, because you have taught rebellion against the Lord.'" So Hananiah the prophet died the same year in the seventh month (Jeremiah 28:15-17).

God typically doesn't strike down false prophets today, but Judgment Day is coming.

WHY TRUE PROPHETS ARE SO OFFENSIVE

Throughout the pages of Scripture, we see true prophets offending God's people. As a result, the prophets were persecuted—and even killed. Think about it. If the prophets would have offered a feel-good message in the name of God, they would have been celebrated. But they told the truth and were persecuted. Isaiah was sawn in two. Jeremiah was thrown into a pit. Micaiah was imprisoned. John the Baptist was beheaded. And Jesus was crucified.

Jesus, the Prophet, offended many religious leaders in His day. In fact, it was so obvious they were offended that His disciples—who often lacked discernment and good judgment—clearly saw it. They came to Jesus after one of His messages, saying, "Do You know that the Pharisees were offended when they heard this saying?" (Matt. 15:12). Jesus proved He was a prophet through His miracles before He proved He was the Messiah by rising from the dead. Still, people familiar with Him were offended.

When He had come to His own country, He taught them in their synagogue, so that they were astonished and said, "Where did this Man get this wisdom and these mighty works? Is this not the carpenter's son? Is not His mother called Mary? And His brothers James, Joses, Simon, and Judas? And His sisters, are they not all with us? Where then did this Man get all these things?" So they were offended at Him. But Jesus said to them, "A prophet is not without honor except in his own country and in his own house." Now He did not do many mighty works there because of their unbelief (Matthew 13:54-58).

At one point, even Jesus' own disciples got offended with Him. He was teaching about the bread that comes down from heaven and let everyone know He was that bread and could bring eternal life. Of course, He was speaking in a parable, as He often did. John 6:60-61 relates, "Therefore many of His disciples, when they heard this, said, 'This is a hard saying; who can understand it?' When Jesus knew in Himself that His disciples complained about this, He said to them, 'Does this offend you?'" Finally, Jesus said, "And blessed is he who is not offended because of Me" (Matt. 11:6).

Why was Jesus—and why are true prophets—so offensive? It's usually not because they are trying to be. No, it's because the truth offends people, which makes no sense. Why would the truth offend us? Jesus described Himself as the truth (see John 14:6), but it's that truth—when we know it—that sets us free (see John 8:32). Lies and deception, by contrast, put us into bondage. The truth sanctifies us (see John 17:17.) Lies, by contrast, defile us. As part of our spiritual armor, God gave us the belt of truth and calls us to speak the truth in love (see Eph. 4:15).

ENEMIES OF TRUTH

Paul wrote a letter to the church at Galatia—a church that seemed to have a problem with the religious spirit. Although they received salvation through grace by faith, they started giving ear to the Judaizers who insisted on following works to be saved. These were false teachers and Paul told the Galatians they were foolish to listen to them (see Gal. 3:1).

Apparently, the Galatians didn't like the truth. Paul wrote, "Have I now become your enemy because I am telling you the truth? Those false teachers are so eager to win your favor, but their intentions are not good. They are trying to shut you off from me so that you will pay attention only to them" (Gal. 4:16-17 NLT).

Paul's letter to the Galatians demonstrates how quickly and easily believers fall prey to false teachers. It's the same with false prophets. The gospel is so simple and every single one of the many thousands of promises in the Bible are yes and amen (see 2 Cor. 1:20). Sometimes, though, we don't want to hear the truth. We'd rather hear a lie that comforts us. And false prophets are right there to oblige.

While true prophets were persecuted in the Old Testament, people loved to hear prophetic witchcraft utterances from false prophets. God released a strong prophecy through several prophets about the false ones who refused to tell Israel the truth.

By lying to God's chosen people, Israel avoided repentance but did not avert disaster. It's the same today. Prophetic witchcraft is wrapped in lies that sometimes sound good to our natural ears. But they grieve God's Spirit. This is a long passage, but one that demonstrates how God feels about prophets and prophetic witchcraft that misleads God's people and even leads them into idolatry.

HOW OFFENSIVE IS PROPHETIC WITCHCRAFT?

In Ezekiel 13:1-2 we read part of the problem:

> *And the word of the Lord came to me, saying, "Son of man, prophesy against the prophets of Israel who prophesy, and say to those who prophesy out of their own heart, 'Hear the word of the Lord!'"*

Notice the indictment. They are prophesying out of their own heart. That means, as the New Living Translation puts it, they "are inventing their own prophecies." Prophetic witchcraft is manufactured, but not in heaven. It's manufactured out of a spirit of manipulation and lying. Ezekiel 13:3-7 continues:

> *Thus says the Lord God: "Woe to the foolish prophets, who follow their own spirit and have seen nothing! O Israel, your prophets are like foxes in the deserts. You have not gone up into the gaps to build a wall for the house of Israel to stand in battle on the day of the Lord. They have envisioned futility and false divination, saying, 'Thus says the Lord!' But the Lord has not sent them; yet they hope that the word may be confirmed. Have you not seen a futile vision, and have you not spoken false divination? You say, 'The Lord says,' but I have not spoken."*

Notice these prophets were not standing in the gap in prayer. God was looking for a man to stand in the gap and make up a hedge so He would not have to release judgment (see Ezek. 22:30). But He couldn't find one. These false prophets not only refused to stand in the gap, they refused to stand for the truth because it wasn't a popular message. They weren't on assignment from the Lord. They spewed predictions steeped prophetic witchcraft—and they actually expected the Lord to back up their utterance. Yes, really!

Ezekiel 13:8-9 goes on:

> *Therefore thus says the Lord God: "Because you have spoken nonsense and envisioned lies, therefore I am indeed against you," says the Lord God. "My hand will be against the prophets who envision futility and who divine lies; they shall not be in the assembly of My people, nor be written in the record of the house of Israel, nor shall they enter into the land of Israel. Then you shall know that I am the Lord God."*

Catch that. God is against prophetic witchcraft. God promised to evict them from the land.

> *Because, indeed, because they have seduced My people, saying, "Peace!" when there is no peace—and one builds a wall, and they plaster it with untempered mortar—say to those who plaster it with untempered mortar, that it will fall. There will be flooding rain, and you, O great hailstones, shall fall; and a stormy wind shall tear it down. Surely, when the wall has fallen, will it not be said to you, "Where is the mortar with which you plastered it?" (Ezekiel 13:10-12)*

Now we get deeper into God's issue. Now we understand better what offends His heart. It was bad enough that they were inventing prophecies. But their inventions defied His Word. They were essentially calling God—and His true servants the prophets—a liar. It was offensive to God's heart because these diviners were setting up His chosen nation for a great fall. Ezekiel was outnumbered, and the voice of prophetic witchcraft dominated Israel's headlines.

Ezekiel 13:13-16 continues:

> *Therefore thus says the Lord God: "I will cause a stormy wind to break forth in My fury; and there shall be a flooding rain in My anger, and great hailstones in fury to consume it. So I will break down the wall you have plastered with untempered mortar, and bring it down to the ground, so that its foundation will be uncovered; it will fall, and you shall be consumed in the midst of it. Then you shall know that I am the Lord.*
>
> *"Thus will I accomplish My wrath on the wall and on those who have plastered it with untempered mortar; and I will say to you, 'The wall is no more, nor those who plastered it, that is, the prophets of Israel who prophesy concerning Jerusalem, and who see visions of peace for her when there is no peace,'" says the Lord God.*

Prophetic witchcraft offends God. It should offend you. Don't believe it. Expose it. Let me assure you. It's dangerous to align with prophetic witchcraft.

CHAPTER 3

THE DANGER IN ALIGNING WITH PROPHETIC
WITCHCRAFT

W e split ways. I had been running hard in an apostolic-pro-phetic partnership and the enemy came in with prophetic witchcraft and blew up the relationship. Neither one of us discerned it at the time. But the enemy planted seed after seed that rose up as trees of division.

Honestly, I was shocked and upset with the loss of this long-term relationship, but when you are in full-time ministry you can't just shut down all the work and hide because you're grieving. You can slow down, but you can't shut down. As I was processing through the loss, the Holy Spirit told me He was birthing unusual partnerships—and I announced this as a word for many who had seen seasons shift in their life.

Specifically, I saw especially unusual partnerships—partnerships that would make people look twice and think again. I saw partnerships between people you would not expect to lock arms. The Holy Spirit said, "Look for the divine connections. Look for the unusual partnerships.

EXPOSING PROPHETIC WITCHCRAFT

Don't think about it in your mind but begin to know each other by the spirit because I am going to birth through you collectively more than what you could birth alone."

That was a hopeful word for many—and I pressed into it for myself. Of course, because I released it publicly many people started trying to connect with me. They felt the unusual partnership was between them and me. Some of the people who reached out were honest and sincere, but not called to walk with me. Others were dishonest deceivers who were blatantly opportunistic and easy to discern. But there were two who were slick, sly, clever, and crafty like the snake in the garden.

One of the snakes was a young man, we'll call him Jack, who was wounded by a spiritual father. I had known him and saw him as gifted, but also discerned he was carrying a load of rejection and other spiritual issues that made him untrustworthy. Still, he reached out at 4 a.m. in absolute desperation for help. I prayed, and the Holy Spirit told me to help him.

And so I did. And he was making progress. He was receiving deliverance from a lot of the pain of his past. He was finding restoration. During this time, he drew close to a man we'll call Ralph. Ralph was extremely charismatic. He was operating in an anointing that caused people to vibrate all the way down to the ground under what appeared to be the power of the Holy Spirit. He seemed to have a gentle spirit— and he wanted to connect with me.

I wasn't sure about Ralph, so I asked Jack. Jack had nothing but high praises for Ralph and encouraged me to connect. Because I was vulnerable from the loss of a ministry partner and because I had a word about unusual partnerships (and this would certainly be an unusual partnership), I proceeded with caution. And I'm glad I did. Just one event into the budding collaboration, I saw so much prophetic witchcraft I severed the cord immediately.

Unfortunately, I lost several thousand dollars in his dishonest process. But the money lost was a valuable lesson. After I severed that cord, young people all over the church world started leaving this man's ministry. He cursed them on the way out the door—literally curses of their ministries falling apart in thirty days, their marriages souring, their finances drying up, and more. I'm sure Ralph was cursing me, too, but a curse causeless shall not land on its intended victim (see Prov. 26:2).

In the end, the young man, Jack, also fell into great deception because he did not disconnect from Ralph. Jack flew to foreign nations to receive impartations from known false prophets. Jack started visibly going off the deep end of divination, releasing curses and judgments publicly against people who dared questioned him. It wasn't long before leaders in the Body of Christ were calling me asking me what happened to him and telling me what I already knew—he had fallen headlong into prophetic witchcraft.

I escaped the danger of aligning with prophetic witchcraft, but Jack didn't. And many others don't either. If you have aligned with prophetic witchcraft, you, too, need to sever the cord and repent. Yes, there will be warfare on the way out the door. But Jesus is your Door and your Strong Tower. You can run to Him and be safe (see Prov. 18:10). And here's a scarier truth: when you align with prophetic witchcraft, some of the blood of the innocent that spills is on your hands. But hold that thought. We'll look more at that in a minute.

WHAT IS PROPHETIC ALIGNMENT?

You may not be familiar with the word *alignment*. It's used in apostolic-prophetic circles as an alternative to the word *covering*. The right connections or alignments can bring great benefits to your life. The wrong alignments or connections can bring warfare or, worse, defile you. Alignment is what keeps your car driving in a straight line. Spiritual alignment can either benefit or hinder your forward-moving progress.

We find the word *alignment* in the New Testament 13 times in the form of the Greek word *katartizo*. According to *The NAS New Testament Greek Lexicon*, it means "to render, i.e. to fit, sound, complete; mend (what has been broken or rent), to repair; to complete; to fit out, equip, put in order, arrange, adjust; and ethically to strengthen, perfect, complete, and make one what he ought to be."

In the context of the "covering" discussion, Scriptures include Ephesians 4:11-12: "And He Himself gave some to be apostles, some prophets, some evangelists, and some pastors and teachers, for the equipping of the saints for the work of ministry, for the edifying of the body of Christ." The word *equipping* is *katartizo*. Consider how the fivefold prophet's primary function is to equip—to ethically strengthen—the saints. When you enter a wrong prophetic alignment—when you deal with prophetic witchcraft—it skews your prophetic ethics. (You can read more about prophetic ethics in my book *Prophetic Ethics and Protocols*.)

Then there's Luke 6:40: "A disciple is not above his teacher, but everyone who is perfectly trained will be like his teacher." The key word here is *trained*, which is *katartizo*. The teacher, or in this case the equipping prophet you are aligned with—the one from whom you learn—will reproduce in you whatever he carries. You may have seen spiritual sons and daughters who carry the movement or the sound or the phrases and styles of their teacher. If you align with prophetic witchcraft, you will carry a wrong spirit.

Let me share a very practical story. I used to live in a condo on the beach. From my office and my balcony—which had floor-to-ceiling windows—I could see the ocean. I loved my time there, except for one memory—the cockroach infestation. See, I was traveling around the world at the time and was only home a few days a week.

After one long trip, I discovered there were cockroaches everywhere. They were crawling around like they owned the place. It was beyond disgusting. I called the management office and told them about the issue. There was no logical reason for this, because the exterminator came once a month like clockwork. My daughter had already moved out, so there were no Cheetos under the couch. As a matter of fact, I had gotten rid of all of my furniture and was waiting for new furniture to arrive, so there weren't too many places for the buggers to hide. My house was clean. Again, it made no sense.

The exterminator came and sprayed an extra time before I headed off to the next trip. When I came home, there were still cockroaches everywhere. I couldn't believe it. It was sickening. A cockroach came out of my printer and was in my coffee pot! I called the management office again and told them about it. They came and sprayed again. I left on another trip, came home and, yes, you guessed it. The condo was overrun with cockroaches.

I got mad with the devil and went to the store to buy bug bombs. I decided to take matters into my own hands to blast these disease-carrying creatures out of my house. I set off the bombs and left overnight. When I came back, it was a roach Armageddon. There were dead bugs everywhere. Though it was gross, I felt a satisfaction. I won!

I left for my next trip feeling satisfied. But when I came home roaches were crawling everywhere. Now I wasn't just mad with the devil, I was mad with the management office. I pay too much in condo fees to live in a roach den. Management agreed to send out an expert. Finally! The exterminator could find no natural reason for it—until he went into the empty unit above mine. It seems the Canadian snowbirds who owned the condo upstairs had been gone for months but had left food out and it was rotten, and the roaches were having a field day. Their condo was completely infested.

What did that have to do with me? The exterminator told me this: "Your wall is aligned with the unit upstairs"—yes, he used those words—"and because you are connected, the roaches are coming from their home to yours." I couldn't believe it. I wasn't even intentionally aligned with them. It was an accidental alignment. And I was suffering because of it. Eventually, I moved out.

PROPHETIC WITCHCRAFT DEFILES YOU

The alignment with my roach-infested neighbors was defiling my house. Prophetic witchcraft will defile you. God doesn't want us to fall into a pit of witchcraft. He warned His people, "Give no regard to mediums and familiar spirits; do not seek after them, to be defiled by them: I am the Lord your God" (Lev. 19:31).

Catch that. Prophetic witchcraft defiles you. The Contemporary English Version of this Scripture reads, "Don't make yourselves disgusting to me by going to people who claim they can talk to the dead." And *The Message* puts it this way: "Don't dabble in the occult or traffic with mediums; you'll pollute your souls. I am God, your God."

Defile means "to make unclean or impure." It means "to corrupt." It means "to contaminate." God calls us to be holy even as He is holy. Prophetic witchcraft and holiness do not mix. True prophets pursue holiness and teach others to do the same. Ezekiel 44:23 tells us, "And they shall teach My people the difference between the holy and the unholy, and cause them to discern between the unclean and the clean."

When the Lord exposes prophetic witchcraft to you and you ignore His warnings, you come under the deception of prophetic witchcraft and it defiles you. Some of the spirit that's on them begins to influence you—and it's not the spirit of Holy. Be sure, the Holy Spirit always warns us when there are counterfeit prophetic operations in our midst. He expects us to discern His warnings of prophetic witchcraft. It's our responsibility to pick up on His warnings. (For more on this, read my book *Discerning Prophetic Witchcraft*.)

"Make no friendship with an angry man, and with a furious man do not go, lest you learn his ways and set a snare for your soul," Solomon wrote in Proverbs 22:24-25. If you can learn the ways of an angry man, you can learn his ways of witchcraft. I'm convinced those who operate in prophetic witchcraft reproduce after their own kind. Maybe they were taught some of the evil practices that defiled them, but that doesn't mean you need to let that teaching defile you. Remember, a little leaven leavens the whole lump (see 1 Cor. 5:6).

David wrote, "Blessed is the man who walks not in the counsel of the ungodly, nor stands in the path of sinners, nor sits in the seat of the scornful" (Ps. 1:1). Looking at this from the contrary view, walking in the counsel of the ungodly and standing in the path of prophetic witchcraft can bring curses in your life. God is certainly not cursing you, but when you are opening yourself up to demons and when you finally cut the cord, prophetic witchcraft operators will curse you on the way out.

DON'T PARTNER WITH PROPHETIC WITCHCRAFT

When you align yourself with someone operating in prophetic witchcraft, you are partnering in the evil work. I am not the one saying this. It's the Word of God.

> *If anyone comes to your meeting and does not teach the truth*
> *about Christ, don't invite that person into your home or give*
> *any kind of encouragement. Anyone who encourages such people*
> *becomes a partner in their evil work* (2 John 1:10-11 NLT).

The Message puts it this way: "If anyone shows up who doesn't hold to this teaching, don't invite him in and give him the run of the place. That would just give him a platform to perpetuate his evil ways, making you his partner." Let that sink in. We have to discern the teaching, but it's not enough to discern it. You have to expose it or you're partnering with it.

Every time we like or share social media laced with prophetic witchcraft, we are partnering with evil work. Every time we sow into a ministry that's operating in prophetic witchcraft, we are partnering with evil work. Every time we buy a book written by someone propagating prophetic witchcraft, we are partnering with evil work. Again, we have to discern the teaching, but it's not just enough to discern it. We have to warn others. This two-step process of discern and expose is found in Ephesians 5:6-13:

> *Let no one deceive you with empty words, for because of these*
> *things the wrath of God comes upon the sons of disobedience.*
> *Therefore do not be partakers with them. For you were once*
> *darkness, but now you are light in the Lord. Walk as children*
> *of light (for the fruit of the Spirit is in all goodness, righteous-*
> *ness, and truth), finding out what is acceptable to the Lord.*
> *And have no fellowship with the unfruitful works of darkness,*
> *but rather expose them. For it is shameful even to speak of*
> *those things which are done by them in secret. But all things*
> *that are exposed are made manifest by the light, for whatever*
> *makes manifest is light.*

I'm not saying to make a blanket statement on Facebook about a false prophet, but when you are walking with friends and family and you see them walking into a prophetic witchcraft trap and don't warn them, some of the blood may be on your hands. The Word of God tells us to expose these things, but many times we're afraid people will not agree with us or cut us off. Maybe we're afraid of the one operating in prophetic witchcraft. But we need to obey the Word of God lest we fall into deception ourselves through hearing and not doing.

Paul assured us light does not have fellowship with darkness (see 2 Cor. 6:14). Paul also reminded us that evil company corrupts good morals (see 1 Cor. 15:33). For his part, Solomon made it known that the companion of fools would get into trouble (see Prov. 13:20). You're asking for trouble when you partner with prophetic witchcraft. Your health may be compromised. Your marriage may fall apart. Your finances may dry up. You may even feel like you are losing your mind. Partnering with evil leads to nothing good.

EXPOSING PROPHETIC WITCHCRAFT ALIGNMENTS

Begin to ask the Holy Spirit to expose prophetic witchcraft alignments in your life. Not everybody has such alignments. Many believers are in strong churches or networks and growing in the grace of God. But if you discern any of these issues in your life but are not sure the source of the trouble, ask the Holy Spirit to expose it so you can find deliverance from it. As I always say, "An enemy exposed is an enemy defeated." You don't have to experience all of these things to conclude you are aligned with prophetic witchcraft. But usually multiple signs will manifest if you pay attention.

EXPOSING PROPHETIC WITCHCRAFT

1. You feel something is off with a person.

You may not discern what is going on, but this is one way the Holy Spirit alerts you to a poor or bad alignment. If it doesn't feel right, it probably isn't. Just because you can't figure out what the matter is doesn't mean you should ignore the matter. Ask the Holy Spirit to show you the matter, knowing that our own biases and past experiences can cloud our judgment. We're not going on a witch hunt here. We're looking to expose wrong associations that let the cockroaches into our life.

2. You feel like your life is being pulled off track.

If you've ever driven a car that's out of alignment, you'll notice it's a struggle to drive down the middle of the road. It's hard to steer steady. The car wants to veer to the right or the left. It takes a lot of energy and concentration to keep the car steady. Meanwhile, you're using more gas and wearing out your tires.

When you feel like certain associations are pulling your life off track, it's a clue of a bad alignment. Prophetic witchcraft alignments will pull you off the narrow path Christ calls us to walk. Jesus said, "Enter by the narrow gate; for wide is the gate and broad is the way that leads to destruction, and there are many who go in by it" (Matt. 7:13). It's tempting to go down the broad path because it seems easier. Prophetic witchcraft operators make a lot of promises about God fast-tracking success, but in the end they are derailing your destiny. Don't fall for it.

3. You feel tempted into loose living.

Again using the car analogy, a bad alignment is often marked by a loose steering wheel. When the steering wheel is loose, it takes longer to respond to danger on the road. When the prodigal son deceived himself, the Bible said he squandered his inheritance in "loose living" (see Luke 15:13 NASB95). Other translations say wild living, reckless living, riotous living, immoral living, and foolish living. Prophetic witchcraft alignments will lead you into a lifestyle that does not glorify God. Thankfully, we can repent, as did the prodigal son.

4. You see a shaking in your life.

The car analogy is so useful here, we'll continue exploring the parallels. When your car is badly out of alignment, your steering wheel starts to shake. When you continue in a prophetic witchcraft alignment, you'll start seeing shakings in your life. While the enemy can seek to shake us without a bad alignment—we all face trials and tribulations—the difference is that a prophetic witchcraft alignment results in a shaking that doesn't stop.

The reason the shaking doesn't stop is because God is trying to shake you to wake you. He's trying to get your attention. He wants you to shake yourself loose from the prophetic witchcraft. You may be crying out to God to stop the shaking, but when you are aligned with prophetic witchcraft, He doesn't answer that prayer. The shaking will stop when you pray a prayer of repentance.

The scary part here, though, is the shaking may also stop if you decide to continually ignore the warnings of the Lord. "If we say that we have no sin, we deceive ourselves" (1 John 1:8). Those in the prophetic witchcraft camp will insist it's an enemy attack, when it reality it's the hand of the Lord. Shaking is an invitation for you to examine your mind and your alignments.

5. You are carrying too much weight.

Automobile experts are quick to tell you that if you have too much weight in the car it can throw off your alignment. Prophetic witchcraft operators will load you up with far more work than you can handle in the name of "service unto the Lord." You will find yourself exhausted because there's no grace to run a race God didn't tell you to enter.

Hebrews 12:1 warns, "Therefore we also, since we are surrounded by so great a cloud of witnesses, let us lay aside every weight, and the sin which so easily ensnares us, and let us run with endurance the race that is set before us." Jesus' burden is easy and His yoke is light (see Matt. 11:28-30). When you are yoked to someone operating in prophetic witchcraft, you are not just burdened—you feel crushed by the burden. It's called oppression.

Maybe it seemed exciting when you were first chosen to carry the load, but now it's overwhelming and there seems to be no way of escape. You feel trapped in a cycle, faced with unreasonable demands on your time, your money, and anything else you have to give.

6. You feel like you've lost yourself.

In a bad prophetic alignment, you may feel like you've lost yourself. And you may have actually lost parts of yourself. You aren't excited about the things of God anymore. Rather, they have become dreaded chores. If you are in a church where prophetic witchcraft is reigning, you may feel like you are entering a war zone—and with good reason. You are getting hit with so-called "friendly fire," when the church is controlling to the point that you can't make a move without their approval and they usually offer disapproval, scrutiny, and downright rebuke.

After I got saved, the Lord told me I would have a prison ministry one day. A couple of years later, I met a woman in a church I attended who was active in the local jail and invited me to come along. I was so excited. I didn't think to ask permission, because it didn't affect the ministry or interfere with anything I was doing for them.

Right before my first day to minister in the jail, the pastor brought me in her office and rebuked me harshly, using the words, "How dare you!" I left her office, got in my car, and cried all the way to the jail. Soon after that, someone from the church started telling the prison chaplain lies about me and forced me out of the ministry. I felt like someone had died. I lost something that day.

7. You feel disconnected from God.

When you feel disconnected from God, there could be many reasons. But make no mistake. Aligning with prophetic witchcraft makes it more difficult to hear the voice of God and makes it more difficult to discern the presence of God. You may not feel like reading the Word, praying, or going to church.

8. Nothing you put your hand to prospers.

The Bible promises everything we put our hand to shall prosper (see Deut. 15:10) and that no weapon formed against us shall prosper (see Isa. 54:17). These are great and precious promises, but they are hindered when you align with prophetic witchcraft.

We see why when we examine Third John 2: "Beloved, I pray that you may prosper in all things and be in health, just as your soul prospers." Your soul isn't prospering when you are aligned with prophetic witchcraft. Rather, your mind is being renewed to lies. Your will is being bent the wrong way. And your emotions are affected.

9. You are constantly experiencing witchcraft attacks.

We'll talk more about that in Chapter 8, "Signs You Are Under a Prophetic Witchcraft Attack."

10. You feel like you are living under a curse.

It may seem that everything that can go wrong does go wrong. Instead of blessings you may see what appear to be curses of disobedience, listed in Deuteronomy 28, because you yoked yourself to the power of the enemy. You may experience unexpected expenses that force you into debt, physical ailments, enemy attacks, confusion, frustration, or the feeling like your prayers are hitting the ceiling.

11. You are afraid to disconnect.

Because prophetic witchcraft intimidates, you may be afraid to disconnect. I remember a church I was in that saw people leave frequently. Every time someone visible left, the pastors cursed them from the pulpit. They told the congregation they were filled with rejection and fear and had backslidden. In reality, they escaped to freedom. If you are afraid to leave a ministry because of the backlash, that's all the more reason to leave.

12. You are emotionally numb.

Emotional numbness can manifest as an emptiness or even a despondency. You may feel isolated and alone, like you are observing everything but it's not really happening to you. You're going through the motions just trying to survive. You are unfocused. This usually stems from ongoing, overwhelming stress, which can lead to anxiety and depression and your efforts to shut down or shut out other feelings.

13. Other people are warning you.

When I was in a toxic church, my family warned me things weren't right. But I didn't believe them at first. Perhaps I didn't want to believe them. When you are aligned with prophetic witchcraft it can be difficult to accept the truth. It may take time to process through it. Usually, others who share the alignment can't see it either so you need outside voices to help you discern.

If you've ever put off taking your car to the mechanic to have it re-aligned, you know how costly it is. The longer you drive your car when it's out of alignment, the more damage it does to the tires and the vehicle. As with a vehicle, there is danger in allowing your life to remain out of alignment. If you sense you are out of alignment, press in and ask God to show you who or what you are aligned to. Align yourself to the Word and to the Spirit. He is faithful to show us what we need to see when we seek Him.

CHAPTER 4

THE RISE OF
FALSE PROPHETS, CHRISTS,
AND ELIJAHS

I was once deceived. Or, you might say, I've been deceived more than once.

Like you, I was deceived before I was saved. My plan was to live however I wanted, repent when I got into my 40s, and start going to church. I figured all would be well with my soul until I was finally ready to stop living in sin. God, in His mercy, had different plans for me. He encountered me in an undeniable way when I was 30, broke the deception, and delivered me from evil.

Soon, though, I fell into another deceptive pit in a hyper-apostolic church that publicly taught "God, family, ministry" but secretly demanded "ministry, ministry, ministry." Our Bibles literally fell open to Ephesians 4:11. And we spelled *apostolic* like this: w-o-r-k. This deception crept in through unbalanced—even extreme—teachings and superhuman expectations that wearied the saints.

When I began to question the status quo, they told me I was deceived. Ironically, I only escaped this abusive church after I began praying for God to break the deception off my mind. See, when the deception accusation came, I knew I was indeed deceived. I just didn't know if I was deceived by the church or deceived by wanting to escape it. Finally, the truth set me free.

Deception—and even the strong delusions that will characterize the end times (see 2 Thess. 2:11)—is already rising in the Body of Christ. And it's far beyond the much-hyped prosperity gospel that mimics New Age philosophies in pursuit of the mighty dollar. Mind you, I'm not against prosperity, and indeed I'm very prosperous. But the love of money is a root of all evil (see 1 Tim. 6:10), and too many prosperity preachers have fallen into deception by getting caught up in the Babylonian paradigm instead of seeking first the Kingdom of God (see Matt. 6:33). Yes, there is a strong delusion manifesting in the church today that goes far beyond the much-hyped prosperity gospel.

How do these (and other) deceptions creep in? And how can you guard yourself from strong delusion? One way is to take heed to the many warnings sounding out from prophetic voices in this generation—and in the Bible. Jesus warned us not to be deceived. Paul warned us not to be deceived. Peter warned us not to be deceived. John warned us not to be deceived. James warned us not to be deceived. You can hardly read a chapter in the New Testament that doesn't issue a warning against deception. And yet deception is dominating some camps in the church.

THE RISE OF FALSE CHRISTS

In the first book in this series, *Discerning Prophetic Witchcraft*, we explored false prophets. But Jesus also warned about false christs: "Take heed that no one deceives you. For many will come in My name, saying, 'I am the Christ,' and will deceive many" (Matt. 24:4-5). And again:

> *Then if anyone says to you, "Look, here is the Christ!" or "There!" do not believe it. For false christs and false prophets will rise and show great signs and wonders to deceive, if possible, even the elect. See, I have told you beforehand. Therefore if they say to you, "Look, He is in the desert!" do not go out; or "Look, He is in the inner rooms!" do not believe it* (Matthew 24:23-26).

I actually met a false christ at a pro-Israel conference in Washington, D.C. I'll never forget the jaw-dropping experience of sitting across from an everyday-Joe-looking filmmaker wearing a blue baseball cap at a popular restaurant when he said, "You are a trustworthy soul, so I am going to confide something to you…I am Jesus Christ."

This man went on to explain, in great detail, how he was reincarnated, why so many reject him as Messiah, and all the supernatural events that confirmed him as the Son of God. I thought he was joking. I felt like I was on *Candid Camera* or in the Twilight Zone. But he was dead serious. I would have thought he was a complete mental case, but he was a semi-successful Christian film producer. I am not sure what causes him to believe with such zeal that he is Christ—or what causes the many other false christs to believe the same.

A little digging shows this false christ syndrome is nothing new. In the 19th century, at least six different men claimed to be Christ. Interestingly, that number swelled in the 20th century. One of the most high-profile "christs" in recent years was Davis Shayler, a former M5 agent and whistleblower who called himself the Messiah in 2007 via YouTube. Then there's Oscar Ramiro Ortega-Hernandez. He claimed to be Jesus Christ on a mission to kill President Obama, whom he considered the antichrist.

Jesus warned, "Then if anyone says to you, 'Look, here is the Christ!' or 'There!' do not believe it. For false christs and false prophets will rise and show great signs and wonders to deceive, if possible, even the elect. See, I have told you beforehand" (Matt. 24:23-25).

Many false christs are indeed rising, but maybe not how we thought. Most of them are easily discernable as whacks and quacks, but a day is coming when false christs will be more convincing. In the meantime, false prophets are serving as the forerunners for the false christs to come. And some of those false prophets are claiming to be Elijah.

THE COMING ELIJAH THEOLOGY

"I have the spirit of Jehu through impartation. I'm John the Baptist," the voice demanded. "I'm Elijah in the flesh." My jaw not only dropped, it fell to the ground when I saw the video of an angry false prophet talking about Jezebel and threatening the window, the ground, or the dogs. He was sending me a message because I had exposed him.

The false prophet was referring to Jehu riding his chariot furiously to command the eunuchs to throw Jezebel down. The Second Kings 9 account shows Jezebel up in a window looking down at the newly minted king before the command came to seize and evict her. The eunuchs threw her out of the window to the ground and the horses trampled her body. Later, dogs devoured her corpse.

I thought, *this fellow is schizophrenic. He doesn't know if he's Jehu, John the Baptist, or Elijah. And he's angrily making threats to release the dogs on people who get in his way, with me first in line.* (This is actually inaccurate biblically because neither Jehu nor Elijah released the dogs. The dogs were not part of Jezebel's demise, but came only after she was rendered powerless.)

This is a dangerous deception and beyond disturbing. What's almost just as disturbing is people were saying "amen" and cheering him on. After I picked my jaw up off the floor, I shut off the broadcast lest I receive a demonic impartation by continuing to let this error flood my eye gates and ear gates. I had to break witchcraft off myself after closing out the screen.

The Elijah deception is not new. Within some segments of the Pentecostal church, people believe that the prophet Elijah will rise up as a forerunner to the Second Coming of Jesus Christ just as John the Baptist rose up as a forerunner to the First Coming of Christ. Remember, Jesus Himself said of John the Baptist, "And if you are willing to receive it, he is Elijah who is to come" (Matt. 11:14).

A few chapters later, Jesus invited John, James, and Peter up to a mountain and He was transfigured. Jesus started talking to Moses and Elijah, and Peter wanted to set up three tents for them. Suddenly, they heard the audible voice of the Father and the fear of the Lord caused them to fall on their faces. Matthew 17:9-13 tells the rest of the story:

> *Now as they came down from the mountain, Jesus commanded them, saying, "Tell the vision to no one until the Son of Man is risen from the dead." And His disciples asked Him, saying, "Why then do the scribes say that Elijah must come first?"*
> *Jesus answered and said to them, "Indeed, Elijah is coming first and will restore all things. But I say to you that Elijah has come already, and they did not know him but did to him whatever they wished. Likewise the Son of Man is also about*

to suffer at their hands." Then the disciples understood that He spoke to them of John the Baptist.

WILL THE REAL ELIJAH PLEASE STAND UP?

John Alexander Dowie, a Scottish-Australian faith healer who immigrated to San Francisco in 1888 before moving to Chicago to leverage the large crowds at the 1893 World's Fair, claimed to be Elijah in the flesh. He quickly amassed thousands of followers, had many homes and businesses—including a publishing company—and purchased an expanse of land to set up Zion, a private Christian community.

Although he was a pioneer in the healing movement long before the Voice of Healing movement in the 20th century—as well as a pioneer in Christian publishing—Dowie had a fatal flaw. Despite his strong biblical beliefs in an end-times restoration of spiritual gifts and apostolic offices that was far ahead of its time, he was in serious error. This goes to show you how you can be very right in many theologies, but dangerously wrong in others.

By 1901, Dowie claimed to be the spiritual return of Elijah from First and Second Kings. He called himself "Elijah the Restorer" and "The Prophet Elijah" and "The Third Elijah." He claimed he was the reincarnation of Elijah the Prophet from Malachi 4:5: "Behold, I will send you Elijah the prophet before the coming of the great and dreadful day of the Lord." During Dowie's time, there were apparently two Elijahs, as Frank Sandford was also known in his own religious cult as Elijah the prophet. This shows you how deep the deception runs—even if one man could have been Elijah, both could not. The people were deceived due to the miracle ministries.

John Collins, author of *Jim Jones: The Malachi 4 Elijah Prophecy,* writes:

> The "Elijah" ministries of these men were not unique, and their claims to being the reincarnation of Biblical prophets were nothing new. Interpreting the ancient Hebrew scroll of the prophecy of Malachi with modern application, ministers such as Dowie and Sandford successfully convinced their listeners that the fourth chapter of Malachi predicted their rise to supernatural power. The doctrinally illiterate, captivated by the charismatic preaching of the ministers, became captives to fear through misuse of their own Bibles. Further amplifying this fear, the "Elijahs" began announcing that the world was ending, and only they knew the hour.[1]

After studying what Dowie and Sandford were doing in their ministries, Charles Fox Parham, one of the founders of modern Pentecost, started a similar healing work. According to Collins, he soon started making his own doomsday predictions and claiming that he, too, was the reincarnated Elijah. Can you see how the spirit of error is contagious? When these men died, the Elijah claims seemed to die with them. But in the 1940s another miracle worker started rising up. His name was William Branham.

ELIJAH CULTS

Branham, the word of knowledge faith healer who amazed many with his gift, started miracle meetings that some say were the foundation for the Latter Rain movement. According to *The Seer's Dictionary*, the Latter Rain movement focused on the baptism of the Holy Spirit, five-fold ministry, the manifestations of the sons of God, and the imminent return of Jesus. The Latter Rain movement taught that God was pouring out His "latter rain" in modern times just as He did on the Day of Pentecost to ready the world for the Second Coming of Christ.

Branham started to view himself as Elijah in the 1960s. Millions believed his claims, dubbing themselves "Message Believers." Branham, who started out with a true gift, ended his life in deception with a prophetic cult that outlived him. Branhamites believe there is no salvation outside of his doctrine. His followers put his teachings above the Word of God.

Jim Jones was ordained into the Latter Rain movement and worked with Branham in 1956. During that series of meetings, Branham prophetically launched Jones into ministry, Collins reports.[2] With Branham's endorsement, which came through a vision of Jones' ministry, Peoples Temple began to grow. Jones, the leader of Peoples Temple, soon began to refer to himself as "Spoken Word" or "Living Word" and claimed he was the reincarnated Elijah.

This is the same Jones who is best known for the mass suicide in 1978 of 914 of its members in Jonestown, Guyana and the murder of five individuals at a nearby airstrip. Over 200 children were murdered at Jonestown, almost all of them by cyanide poisoning.

In more recent years the late Herbert W. Armstrong, founder of the Worldwide Church of God who passed on in 1986, declared he was the end-times Elijah Jesus mentioned in Malachi 4:5-6:

> *Behold, I will send you Elijah the prophet before the coming of the great and dreadful day of the Lord. And he will turn*

the hearts of the fathers to the children, and the hearts of the
children to their fathers, lest I come and strike the earth with
a curse.

One has to ask a serious question: What spirit is motivating some-one to believe that they are the reincarnation of a prophet who walked the earth thousands of years ago? And what spirit is motivating people to believe it?

THE SPIRIT BEHIND FALSE ELIJAHS

Jesus mentioned false prophets and false christs, but did not mention false Elijahs. Still, they are rising and would categorically qualify as false prophets. So what is the spirit behind the false Elijahs? Essentially, it's a spirit of error. The spirit of error opposes the spirit of truth, which is the Holy Spirit (see John 16:13).

John had a revelation of these opposing forces, which is why he warned us in First John 4: "Beloved, do not believe every spirit, but test the spirits, whether they are of God; because many false prophets have gone out into the world" (1 John 4:1). And again, "We are of God. He who knows God hears us; he who is not of God does not hear us. By this we know the spirit of truth and the spirit of error" (1 John 4:6). Depending on what translation you read, it might say a spirit of false-hood, a spirit of deception, a spirit of deceit, or a spirit of lies.

Peter and Paul also warn about a spirit of error. Paul told Timothy, "Now the Spirit expressly says that in latter times some will depart from the faith, giving heed to deceiving spirits and doctrines of demons" (1 Tim. 4:1). And Peter warned:

You therefore, beloved, since you know this beforehand, beware lest you also fall from your own steadfastness, being led away with the error of the wicked (2 Peter 3:17).

For when they speak great swelling words of emptiness, they allure through the lusts of the flesh, through lewdness, the ones who have actually escaped from those who live in error (2 Peter 2:18).

WHEN ERROR TURNS TO HERESY

What starts as a deception can attract a spirit of error that turns into heresy. Heresy is a religious belief or doctrine contrary to standard Christian beliefs, a denial of Bible truth, or actions and practices that are contrary to the generally accepted truth. Heresy is different from error in that one chooses to adopt his own view rather than the standard view. Peter warned:

But false prophets also arose among the people, just as there will be false teachers among you, who will secretly bring in destructive heresies, even denying the Master who bought them, bringing upon themselves swift destruction (2 Peter 2:1 ESV).

Heresies, which usually lead to the formation of sects and splinters of Christianity, have plagued the church through history. The Arians, for example, held the heretical view that Jesus was the Son of God but neither eternal nor divine. Gnostics believe Jesus never took on a body and therefore never physically died on the cross. Pelagians believed good deeds alone get you to heaven. Free Spirits believed man can reach such a state of spiritual perfection that they are above the law.

A Lifeway survey reveals most American Christians are actually heretics. More than half of those surveyed agreed Jesus is "the first and greatest being created by God." This is the heresy of Arianism, which the Council of Nicaea condemned in A.D. 325. Sixty-four percent believe God accepts the worship of all religions, even those who have multiple gods. Two-thirds admitted everyone sins but that most people are good-natured. Seventy-four percent said little sins don't demand eternal damnation. Sixty percent believe everyone goes to heaven, a heresy called Universalism.[3]

Essentially, many believers are uneducated about what the Word of God says, so they are forming their own opinions or just listening to what deceived preachers are telling them. Paul ran into this issue in Galatia, and said, "I marvel that you are turning away so soon from Him who called you in the grace of Christ, to a different gospel, which is not another; but there are some who trouble you and want to pervert the gospel of Christ" (Gal. 1:6-7).

The problem with another gospel is, if you live by it you are serving another Jesus. Paul saw this in his day also:

> *For if he who comes preaches another Jesus whom we have not preached, or if you receive a different spirit which you have not received, or a different gospel which you have not accepted— you may well put up with it!* (2 Corinthians 11:4)

Part of the issue, researchers say, is pastors are just trying to help people get by week by week and do not necessarily offer deeper theology in their messages. The other side of that coin is many believers don't necessarily want theology—the study of God. They want a quick fix to the mess they are in. We are living in the days of Second Timothy 4:3-4:

> *For the time will come when they will not endure sound doctrine, but according to their own desires, because they have itching ears, they will heap up for themselves teachers; and they will turn their ears away from the truth, and be turned aside to fables.*

Paul also warned:

> *For there are many insubordinate, both idle talkers and deceivers, especially those of the circumcision, whose mouths must be stopped, who subvert whole households, teaching things which they ought not, for the sake of dishonest gain* (Titus 1:10-11).

IT'S NOT ALL ABOUT ELIJAH

Deception is a major sign of the last days, and we're seeing deception rise at a rapid clip as megachurch preachers stand before the masses, preach heresy, and sell thousands of books. The saints heap praise on false apostles, false prophets, and false teachers. Pride is driving people, many of whom aren't even called into fivefold ministry, to don extravagant titles like "Official Prophetess" and "Chief Apostle Bishop Dr." and "Master Prophet Bishop." What happened to the bondservants? The lack of discernment in the Body of Christ is disturbing. Where are the lovers of the truth (see 2 Thess. 2:10)?

How do you protect yourself from the spirit of error and heresy? I believe being a student of the Word is one safeguard against deception. Paul told Timothy, "Be diligent to present yourself approved to God, a worker who does not need to be ashamed, rightly dividing the word of truth" (2 Tim. 2:15). Right after that, he spoke of Hymenaeus and Philetus, who had "strayed concerning the truth" and were "saying that the resurrection is already past; and they overthrow the faith of some" (2 Tim. 2:18). In other words, they were preaching a false gospel.

Charismatic heretics are overthrowing the faith of some even now, preaching a false gospel. That's why you can't just be a lover of the Word someone else preaches. You have to study the Word yourself. You have to measure every message you read or hear against the Word of God for yourself. Don't just check to see if the Scripture is in your Bible, but study its meaning in the context of the chapter, book, and entire Bible. When you do, much of the heresy is quickly discerned. But the church at large is lukewarm and lazy, preferring to feast on flashy sermons without lifting a finger to open their own Bibles.

A PRAYER CHALLENGE

I don't have all the answers, but I've been praying about this for years now. I started praying for God to break deception off my mind and to guard me from deception several years ago. Again, I don't have all the answers. But God has granted me discernment to escape much of the "religion" and deception that has risen in the church in this hour. And I am grateful for that grace.

See, the problem with deception is that you don't know you are deceived. If you knew you were deceived, you'd walk away from the lie and embrace the truth. Lovers of the truth are less likely to be deceived, but anyone can fall into deception. And if you think you are above the possibility of falling into deception, you are walking in a deception called pride. So I challenge you—begin to pray for God to break off any deception that has clouded your soul. Beseech Him by His mercy to deliver you from the grip of deception, to shine light on your mind, and to give you discernment.

If you aren't deceived, that prayer won't hurt you. And, in fact, I believe we are all walking in some level of deception—even if it's on minor issues—because our minds are not completely renewed. If our minds were completely renewed, I believe we'd be walking in greater authority and seeing more miracles, signs, and wonders in our lives. In other words, I believe we're all believing something that doesn't completely line up with God's Word.

So, again, I challenge you—I beg you—to begin to pray for God to break off any deception that has clouded your soul. Beseech Him by His mercy to deliver you from the grip of deception, to shine light on your mind, and to give you discernment. You've got nothing to lose by releasing this petition, and you've got possibly your eternal soul to gain as God breaks in with light, exposes the enemy's lies, and sets you free—or protects you—from the strong delusion that sends many to hell. Amen.

NOTES

1. John Collins, "Jim Jones and the Malachi 4 Prophecy of Elijah," Alternative Considerations of Jonestown & Peoples Temple, December 30, 2021, https://jonestown.sdsu.edu/?page _id=70743.

2. Ibid.

3. G. Shane Morris, "Survey Finds Most American Christians Are Actually Heretics," The Federalist, October 10, 2016, https://thefederalist.com/2016/10/10/survey-finds-american-christians-actually-heretics.

CHAPTER 5

EXPOSING FALSE VISIONS, DREAMS, AND
ENCOUNTERS

Heaven is for real, but Alex Malarkey's "true story" about coming back from heaven turned out to be absolutely false. *The Boy Who Came Back from Heaven* was based on fables, tall tales, and all out lies. Malarkey admitted he made up the story of dying and going to heaven after a 2004 car accident that left him in a coma for two months and paralyzed when he finally woke up. The description of the book reads:

> In 2004, Kevin Malarkey and his six-year-old son, Alex, suffered a horrific car accident. The impact from the crash paralyzed Alex—and medically speaking, it was unlikely that he could survive. "I think Alex has gone to be with Jesus," a friend told the stricken dad.
>
> But two months later, Alex awoke from a coma with an incredible story to share. Of events at the accident scene

and in the hospital while he was unconscious. Of the angels that took him through the gates of heaven itself. Of the unearthly music that sounded just terrible to a six-year-old. And, most amazing of all ... Of meeting and talking to Jesus.

The Boy Who Came Back from Heaven is the true story of an ordinary boy's most extraordinary journey. As you see heaven and earth through Alex's eyes, you'll come away with new insights on miracles, life beyond this world, and the power of a father's love.

Malarkey wrote an open letter in 2015 that offered the startling confession:

"Please forgive the brevity, but because of my limitations I have to keep this short. I did not die. I did not go to Heaven." Why did the then-six-year-old boy tell such a tall tale? He explained, "I said I went to heaven because I thought it would get me attention. When I made the claims that I did, I had never read the Bible. People have profited from lies, and continue to. They should read the Bible, which is enough. The Bible is the only source of truth. Anything written by man cannot be infallible."[1]

Lifeway pulled the book after this admission. Malarkey sued Tyndale and rebuked Lifeway for not holding fast to Scripture.

Malarkey is not the first to claim to go to heaven—or to hell—or to talk to Jesus, demons, or angels. Books, TV shows, podcasts, and articles on these topics are beyond popular and many of them are authentic, but it's likely Malarkey is not the only one who has lied. Indeed, too many people have profited and are profiting from false visions, dreams, and encounters. Malarkey exposed his own lie, which shows integrity, and pointed people back to the Bible. But many false visionaries and dreamers continue to propagate stories of fabricated encounters. Nevertheless, we can't write off every dream, vision and encounter because of a few con artists who peddle prophetic rendezvous for profit.

EXPOSING FALSE DREAMS AND VISIONS

God is speaking to people through dreams and visions—and believers are having legitimate encounters with God. In Acts 2:16-18, Peter re-prophesied Joel the prophet's words:

> But this is what was spoken by the prophet Joel: "And it shall come to pass in the last days, says God, that I will pour out of My Spirit on all flesh; your sons and your daughters shall prophesy, your young men shall see visions, your old men shall dream dreams. And on My menservants and on My maidservants I will pour out My Spirit in those days; and they shall prophesy."

With more teaching than ever before on dreams, visions, and encounters—I write about all of this and more in my book *The Seer Dimensions*—the faith of believers everywhere is rising to enter into heavenly realms by the leadership of the Holy Spirit through the door of Jesus. But satan—who masquerades himself as an angel of light (see 2 Cor. 11:14-15)—woos some who seek the supernatural into counterfeit encounters. The problem is, despite all the teaching, many people can't discern between a true and false encounter. They publish their stories on blogs and the false encounter—sometimes encounters that defy Scripture—go viral and deceive many. They spread error in innocent ignorance, but it still does damage.

As mentioned, others absolutely fabricate dreams, visions, and encounters. This is a satanic strategy that is thousands of years old and, despite biblical warnings, is still effective today. God told Jeremiah:

> *I have heard what the prophets have said who prophesy lies in My name, saying, "I have dreamed, I have dreamed!" How long will this be in the heart of the prophets who prophesy lies? Indeed they are prophets of the deceit of their own heart, who try to make My people forget My name by their dreams which everyone tells his neighbor, as their fathers forgot My name for Baal* (Jeremiah 23:25-27).

God also told Jeremiah:

> *This is what the Lord of Heaven's Armies, the God of Israel, says: "Do not let your prophets and fortune-tellers who are with you in the land of Babylon trick you. Do not listen to their dreams, because they are telling you lies in my name. I have not sent them," says the Lord* (Jeremiah 29:8-9 NLT).

This demonic trend of false encounters was vivid in Jeremiah's day. And it's not just dreams. God is also disgruntled with the false visions. God told Jeremiah:

> *The prophets prophesy lies in My name. I have not sent them, commanded them, nor spoken to them; they prophesy to you a false vision, divination, a worthless thing, and the deceit of their heart. Therefore thus says the Lord concerning the prophets who prophesy in My name, whom I did not send, and who say, "Sword and famine shall not be in this land"—By*

sword and famine those prophets shall be consumed! And the people to whom they prophesy shall be cast out in the streets of Jerusalem because of the famine and the sword; they will have no one to bury them—them nor their wives, their sons nor their daughters—for I will pour their wickedness on them (Jeremiah 14:14-16).

It gets even more dangerous when people create doctrine and establish theology based on dreams and visions. While dreams and visions can give us tremendous revelation, some are making every move on dreams and visions people send them—dreams and visions that confirm what they want to hear. Others claim greater authority in the spirit because of their dreams and visions.

Jude talks about these types in Jude 1:8, "In the same way, these people—who claim authority from their dreams—live immoral lives, defy authority, and scoff at supernatural beings" (NLT). *Barnes' Notes on the Bible* expounds on this verse, "Their doctrines were the fruits of mere imagination, foolish vagaries and fancies." Some, for example, are spreading doctrine that allows believers to ascend to the second heaven at will to battle principalities like Leviathan when the Bible clearly states we cannot draw out Leviathan (see Job 41:1). Indeed, many false teachings come out of dreams, visions, and encounters.

So while God is pouring out His spirit, the enemy is up to the same old tricks. He's convincing people to fabricate encounters for the sake of platform, popularity, and paychecks. The enemy is tempting people to manufacture dreams and visions to elevate themselves as somehow more spiritual than others.

Still, just as we should not despise prophecy (see 1 Thess. 5:20), we should not despise dreams, visions, and encounters. We just test all things and hold fast to that which is good (see 1 Thess. 5:21). We must not automatically believe every prophet. We have to test the spirits because the false is rising (see 1 John 4:1). But we can't throw out the supernatural because of a few false fruits, flakes, and nuts.

EXPOSING FALSE ANGELIC ENCOUNTERS

Angelic encounters are on the rise—even secular news media are reporting stories of activity among the heavenly hosts. Wise ones proceed with caution, though, because Scripture clearly warns satan himself masquerades as an angel of light (see 2 Cor. 11:14).

Still, there's another issue of concern in the Body of Christ: prophets and prophetic people, among others, flat-out lying about seeing angels. Of course, like most deceptions that run rampant in the church today, this practice dates back many thousands of years.

Indeed, angelic deceptions are nothing new, but it seems the false is rising with the true—and the fabricated are rising with the false. Discernment has never been more vital. Take it from a young prophet who lost his life after he believed an elder prophet's lie about an angel.

We read the account in First Kings 13. A young man of God prophesied against King Jeroboam, who had fallen from grace. Jeroboam ordered his arrest, only to watch his arm wither. After the young prophet prayed for the king and his arm was restored, Jeroboam offered him a reward.

The man of God said to the king, "If you were to give me half your house, I would not go with you, nor will I eat bread nor drink water in this place, for so I was commanded by the word of the Lord, saying: You shall eat no bread, nor drink water nor return by the same way that you came." So he went another way and did not return by the same way he came to Bethel (1 Kings 13:8-10 MEV).

Now, the sons of an elder prophet were duly impressed. They went home and told dad everything the young prophet said to the king. The old prophet went after him with deception in his heart. We read this in First Kings 13:15-19:

> *Then he said to him, "Come home with me and eat bread." He said, "I may not return with you or go in with you, nor will I eat bread nor drink water with you in this place, for I was commanded by the word of the Lord: You shall eat no bread and drink no water there nor return by the way you came." He said to him, "I am a prophet like you, and an angel spoke to me by the word of the Lord, saying, 'Bring him back with you into your house so that he may eat bread and drink water.'" But he had lied to him. So he went back with him to his house and ate bread and drank water* (MEV).

The fate of this young prophet: his disobedience left him dead at the hand of a lion. Although this young prophet was staunchly obedient to God in his assignment to prophesy against a wicked king, he was deceived by an elder prophet's false angelic visitation. Let that be a warning to you—and consider how entirely false religions have been based on angelic encounters.

FALSE ENCOUNTERS BIRTH FALSE THEOLOGY

Within Christianity, we see many theological errors arising from false dreams, visions, and counters. That's dangerous enough, but when you consider false dreams, visions, and encounters have birthed entirely false religions that send people to hell, you can better appreciate the danger. Sure, we won't go to hell for sowing into a false prophet or false teacher with extreme theology based on made-up encounters, but it opens us up to deep deception and, at times, even sin.

The Church of Jesus Christ of Latter-Day Saints, long-known as Mormonism, is based on an encounter with a false angel. Mormonism founder Joseph Smith chronicled his false encounter in 1823. As recorded, he encountered an angel named Moroni in his bedroom, surrounded in brilliant light. This angel reportedly prophesied to Smith about a great work, pointed to the Book of Isaiah, and quoted other Scripture passages, then warned Smith not to show anyone the golden plates on which the Book of Mormon was written. Moroni allegedly visited Smith three times in one night.

Smith wrote, "The fundamental principles of our religion are... concerning Jesus Christ, that He died, was buried, and rose again the third day, and ascended into heaven; and all other things which pertain to our religion are only appendages to it."[2] But Mormons also say Father God was not always God, that He was not the Creator but was Himself created. Mormons believe there are levels of heaven we attain based on works. Mormons believe Jesus was birthed through a physical relationship between God the Father and Mary. All of this defies Scripture.

A man named Muhammad, who claimed to be a prophet, founded Islam in A.D. 610 based on an angelic encounter. PBS reports:

According to Muslim belief, at the age of 40, Muhammad is visited by the angel Gabriel while on retreat in a cave near Mecca. The angel recites to him the first revelations of the Quran and informs him that he is God's prophet. Later, Muhammad is told to call his people to the worship of the one God, but they react with hostility and begin to persecute him and his followers.[3]

Encyclopedia Britannica continues:

> The archangel Gabriel brought the Qur'ān down to the Prophet's "heart." Gabriel is represented by the Qur'ān as a spirit whom the Prophet could sometimes see and hear. According to early traditions, the Prophet's revelations occurred in a state of trance when his normal consciousness was transformed. This state was accompanied by heavy sweating. The Qur'ān itself makes it clear that the revelations brought with them a sense of extraordinary weight: "If we were to send this Qur'ān down on a mountain, you would see it split asunder out of fear of God."[4]

Muslims do not believe in the deity or the crucifixion of Jesus Christ. Muslims believe Jesus was fully man and respect Him as a prophet, but not the Son of God. This flies in the face of Scripture. Yet Islam is the fastest-growing religion in the world—and, again, it was birthed from a false angelic visitation. Whether or not Muhammad made up the story or an angel of light visited him, we do not know.

In more recent years, Jose Luis de Jesus Miranda, a heretic with a 666 tattoo who claimed to be the Messiah, says he discovered he was Christ after angels visited him in a dream. CNN reported his key messages:

there is no devil and no sin and we can do no wrong in God's mind.[5] At the same time, false messiahs are rising around the world. As legitimate angelic encounters increase, it's important to remember as we open our eyes to the reality of angels that no angel replaces the Holy Spirit or contradicts the Word of God.

Paul had plenty to say about false angelic messages and those who deliver them.

> *Do not let anyone cheat you of your reward by delighting in false humility and the worship of angels, dwelling on those things which he has not seen, vainly arrogant due to his unspiritual mind, and not supporting the head, from which the entire body, nourished and knit together by joints and sinews, grows as God gives the increase* (Colossians 2:18-19 MEV).

Any true message from an angel will support the head—Jesus. Jesus is the head of the angels—the Captain of the hosts—and the head of the church. Just as we must judge prophecy, we must judge messages from angels through a prophet. Many false doctrines and false religions have been propagated by people who claim an angelic messenger visited them. Paul said in Galatians 1:6-9:

> *I marvel that you are turning away so soon from Him who called you in the grace of Christ to a different gospel, which is not a gospel. But there are some who trouble you and would pervert the gospel of Christ. Although if we or an angel from heaven preach any other gospel to you than the one we have preached to you, let him be accursed. As we said before, so I say now again: If anyone preaches any other gospel to you than the one you have received, let him be accursed* (MEV).

Strong words. There is a rise of authentic angelic activity in the earth. But there is also a rise of the false. Let's not let the roaming lion steal, kill, and destroy our lives like he did the young prophet who fell for the old prophet's angelic deception.

BEWARE MINISTRIES BUILT ON ENCOUNTERS ONLY

It's wearisome. Some apostles, prophets, evangelists, pastors, and teachers have built their entire ministries on supernatural encounters, dreams, visions, and prophecies. Nearly every day, it's a new prophetic prediction, dramatic encounter, or life-changing epiphany. Indeed, some of these purveyors of prophecy seem to walk in more revelation than Paul the apostle himself, except their revelations are anti-biblical. Yes, anti-biblical, not just extra-biblical. It's actually more than wearisome.

I agree not every encounter we could have in the seer dimensions is recorded in the Bible. After all, John wrote plainly that, "There are also many other things that Jesus did, which if they were written one by one, I suppose that even the world itself could not contain the books that would be written" (John 21:25). But the Word and the Spirit agree. The Holy Spirit inspired authors to write Scripture, so He will not violate His own principles and precepts.

The problem is, too few discern embellished, exaggerated, or counterfeit encounters because they are enamored by the dramatic dreams penned with such great literary style that they *just have to be* true! Too few discern the fabricated angelic conversations at the bedside of the prophet because they hunger for the supernatural. This book hopes to change that.

It troubles me how people become overnight superstars based on one concocted encounter that, to the discerning, defies any resemblance to Bible truth. Second heaven dreams have made prophetic celebrities out of people who are no more than fly-by-night fibbers who enjoy the attention. One Facebook post goes viral and they quickly erect a prophetic manufacturing plant that churns out contrived oracles that didn't originate with the Master Orator. It's prophetic witchcraft. We must begin to expose it.

While I believe in angelic encounters, prophecy, dreams, and visions, a generation has risen that makes luminaries out of Christians who behave more like Nostradamus (who was considered a seer in his day)—even when they defy Bible truth. There is popularity in predictions about everything from sporting events to extinct species. (How does that edify the Body of Christ? A psychic can make those predictions.) We must stop tolerating prophetic practices that even get close to the edge of witchcraft and rather embrace the true prophetic word of the Lord, even when it makes us uncomfortable.

DANGER FOR THE UNDISCERNING

This is dangerous for the Body of Christ. It's a leaven that is spreading rapidly. The enemy sowed tares in the field while we were sleeping and now we don't readily discern between the truth and a lie. It's beyond troubling. It's grievous.

Why does this happen? Often, it's because people don't know Bible truth. It's beyond wearisome. It's troubling. Part of it is culture within some camps of Charismatic Christianity that values gifts of the Spirit over the Word of God—or at least puts gifts on par with the Word of God as evidence of someone's spirituality. Many don't discern the motive of the minister is merely to gain a following. I call this "platforms and paychecks." This is not new. It's has been going on since Old Testament times. Paul warned the church:

> *I know that after I leave, imposters who have no loyalty to the flock will come among you like savage wolves. Even some from among your very own ranks will rise up, twisting the truth to seduce people into following them instead of Jesus. So be alert and discerning. Remember that for three years, night and day, I've never stopped warning each of you, pouring out my heart to you with tears* (Acts 20:29-31 TPT).

Judging dreams, visions, and encounters can be a little trickier than judging prophetic words. God can speak to us in a dream language that is very intimate to us. Visions can be partial. Encounters are personalized. Indeed, God has a unique relationship with every one of us and manifests His communications and His heart accordingly. Some people feel the weight of His glory. Others feel tingling in their body. Others don't feel a thing but hear or see dramatic revelations unfolding.

While the Word of God is our baseline for judging encounters—anything that violates the Spirit of the Word is false—the nuances of relational encounters can't always be found in the pages of the Bible. So what do we do? We look at the fruit of the encounter. A true dream, vision, or encounter will exalt Christ in our lives—and the lives of others. A true encounter will draw us closer to His plans and purposes, not into idolatry. A true encounter will cause a change in our thinking and behavior.

In other words, an encounter with God's Spirit will produce the fruit of the Spirit in our lives. Paul writes:

> *But the fruit of the Spirit is love, joy, peace, longsuffering,
> kindness, goodness, faithfulness, gentleness, self-control.
> Against such there is no law. And those who are Christ's have
> crucified the flesh with its passions and desires. If we live in
> the Spirit, let us also walk in the Spirit. Let us not become
> conceited, provoking one another, envying one another* (Gala-
> tians 5:22-26).

Keep this in mind: many encounters, dreams, and visions are
intensely personal. When we apply a personal encounter to the Body
of Christ, we're in error. What is meant for your life is not necessarily
meant for the entire church. And, in any case, what is meant for the
entire church is also relevant to and should be applied to your life before
you broadcast it to the masses.

A WORD TO THE COMPROMISED PROPHETS

If you build your ministry on prophecy, supernatural encounters, and
anything else beyond the Word of God, it won't last. Hear me, as I
speak this truth in love: you can't sustain that level of revelation. You
will begin to miss your predictions of world events, and people will
catch on even if you bury that prophecy in a slew of "accurate" words.
Prophets can make all the excuses in the world why the prophetic word
didn't come to pass; that doesn't mean the word was accurate.

Compromised prophet, you likely have a true gift but you went
astray somewhere in a social media-driven world. Your best move now
would be to back away from the manufacturing plant and begin to
restructure your ministry. Do a top to bottom reorganization. In other
words, change your motives and thought processes and let it trickle

down. Build the foundation of your ministry on the Word. Jesus put it best in Matthew 7:24-27:

> *Therefore whoever hears these sayings of Mine, and does them, I will liken him to a wise man who built his house on the rock: and the rain descended, the floods came, and the winds blew and beat on that house; and it did not fall, for it was founded on the rock. But everyone who hears these sayings of Mine, and does not do them, will be like a foolish man who built his house on the sand: and the rain descended, the floods came, and the winds blew and beat on that house; and it fell. And great was its fall.*

NOTES

1. "'The Boy Who Came Back From Heaven' Recants Story, Rebukes Christian Retailers" Pulpit & Pen, January 13, 2015, https://pulpitandpen.org/2015/01/13/the-boy-who-came-back-from-heaven-recants-story-rebukes-christian-retailers.

2. Joseph Smith, qtd. in "Introduction," The Church of Jesus Christ of Latter-day Saints, https://www.churchofjesuschrist.org/manual/our-heritage/introduction?lang=eng.

3. "Timeline of Islam," PBS.org, http://www.pbs.org/wgbh/pages/frontline/teach/muslims/timeline.html.

4. "Doctrines of the Qur'ān," *Encyclopedia Britannica,* https://www.britannica.com/topic/Islam/Doctrines-of-the-Qur-an.

5. John Zarrella and Patrick Oppmann, "Pastor with 666 tattoo claims to be divine," CNN.com, February 19, 2007, http://www.cnn.com/2007/US/02/16/miami.preacher/index.html?_s=PM:US.

CHAPTER 6

THE SATANIC
ROOTS OF PROPHETIC
WITCHCRAFT

Her name was "Tiny." But the long African rock python outgrew her name. Dan Brandon, an experienced snake owner, let the eight-foot serpent slither around his body and posted pictures of his dangerous poses with the deadly creatures. Brandon felt the python was merely showing its affection. Clearly, the snake deceived him as one day his mother heard a "thud" coming from his room and found him dead. Brandon, then 31, died by asphyxiation.[1]

In my book, *The Spiritual Warrior's Guide to Defeating Water Spirits*, I pondered if the snake satan possessed in the Garden of Eden was a python. We know there was a river running out of Eden to water the Garden that shot off into four riverheads where pythons would dwell. We know God created all creatures and brought them to Adam to name them. We also know the serpent was the shrewdest, most cunning and clever of all the animals God made—but perhaps Adam didn't know it.

I still ponder if the snake in the Garden of Eden was a python because the python spirit is a spirit of divination—essentially prophetic witchcraft. The girl with the spirit of divination in Acts 16 who was prophesying about Paul and Silas was operating in prophetic witchcraft. The words she was saying were accurate but the spirit behind them was putrid.

The Greek word for *divination* in Acts 16:16 is *puthon*. *The KJV New Testament Greek Lexicon* defines *puthon* this way: "In Greek mythology the name of the Pythian serpent or dragon that dwelt in the region of Pytho at the foot of Parnassus in Phocis, and was said to have guarded the oracle at Delphi and been slain by Apollo; a spirit of divination." This is in line with Greek mythology, but clearly Python is more than a myth, as Paul cast the spirit out of the girl.

We see prophetic witchcraft through the pages of the Bible, in the Old and New Testaments, and from Genesis to Revelation, but prophetic witchcraft started in the Garden of Eden. Indeed, prophetic witchcraft has been around since the early days of man—in fact, even before, as lucifer was operating in witchcraft when he sought to rebel against God, and he likely prophesied to the third of the angels who followed him. Clearly, the fallen angels were bewitched, then deceived. The angels knew God was real. They were in His presence. It was a strong delusion. Yes, the angels were bewitched. And so was Eve.

WHEN THE SNAKE PROPHESIES

The snake in the Garden prophesied to Eve. He bewitched her with smooth sayings and compelling false prophecies that beguiled her. The snake started up a conversation with the woman while Adam was out of the immediate picture, demonstrating how prophetic witchcraft seeks out the most vulnerable to deceive. Had the snake tried to prophesy to Adam, I believe he would have run the serpent out of the garden.

The snake targeted Eve, and started with a seemingly innocent question:

> *"Did God really say you must not eat the fruit from any of the trees in the garden?" "Of course we may eat fruit from the trees in the garden," the woman replied. "It's only the fruit from the tree in the middle of the garden that we are not allowed to eat. God said, 'You must not eat it or even touch it; if you do, you will die'"* (Genesis 3:1-3 NLT).

Here, the snake was testing Eve's knowledge of the Word of God to see how vulnerable she really was. This is a common ploy among prophetic witchcraft purveyors. They don't bother with the Christian who knows the Word of God and the ways of God because such believers discern the spirit behind the prophecy and reject the false utterance immediately. Discerning Christians don't fall prey to the flashy gimmicks and flattery because they are rooted and grounded in Christ, the Word made flesh. Satan was testing Eve's knowledge of God's Word and found a hole in her theology.

See, God never told Adam and Eve they could not touch the tree. God's exact words to Adam were, "Of every tree of the garden you may freely eat; but of the tree of the knowledge of good and evil you shall not eat, for in the day that you eat of it you shall surely die" (Gen. 2:16-17). Part of Eve's problem is she has secondhand revelation. Adam heard the command directly from God. Either Adam didn't retell the instruction accurately, leaving Eve vulnerable to the snake's deception, or Eve didn't recall the revelation accurately. Either way, the error opened her up to the enemy's prophetic witchcraft.

The snake saw the weakness and started to twist God's Word with a false prophetic promise:

> *"You won't die!" the serpent replied to the woman. "God knows that your eyes will be opened as soon as you eat it, and you will be like God, knowing both good and evil"* (Genesis 3:4-5 NLT).

Look at how tempting the prophetic witchcraft was. It was a promise of being like God. Eve didn't understand they were already created in the image of God and had been set up as little gods to take dominion over the earth. Satan wanted to be like God and couldn't, so he didn't want Adam and Eve to be like Him either. Satan knew his prophetic word was false and would defile mankind. But Eve did not discern the prophetic witchcraft, which wrapped around the snake's lies.

> *The woman was convinced. She saw that the tree was beautiful and its fruit looked delicious, and she wanted the wisdom it would give her. So she took some of the fruit and ate it. Then she gave some to her husband, who was with her, and he ate it, too. At that moment their eyes were opened, and they suddenly felt shame at their nakedness. So they sewed fig leaves together to cover themselves* (Genesis 3:6-7 NLT).

Prophetic witchcraft led to the fall of man, and still leads to the fall of man in the sense that it pulls its victims out of the will of God. Eve knew she was deceived and admitted it to God, but it was too late to reverse the curse. Thank God, He already had a plan in place to send a true Prophet, Jesus Christ, to redeem us from the curse.

SATAN'S PROPHETIC POWER

Witchcraft is essentially a force, or power, rooted in illegitimate authority. Witchcraft manifests in many ways, including prophetic words. Purveyors of prophetic witchcraft are speaking in the name of Jesus presumptuously—they are operating in a self-proclaimed authority. They are spewing communications originating in the kingdom of darkness and not from God's Kingdom of light, in which there is no darkness.

Just as the Holy Spirit is the power of God to bring change in the lives of people—to bring them into the abundant life Jesus died to give them as they are conformed to His image, to bring healing to the sick, deliverance to the bound, and joy to the mourners—witchcraft is a strong, deceptive force satan uses as a weapon to steal, kill, and destroy (see John 10:10).

Satan does have power on the earth, and witchcraft is part and parcel of that power. But here's what many fail to understand: satan has no real authority beyond what God allows. God is sovereign. Satan cannot do anything without God's permission. We see this in the Book of Job, where satan asked for permission try Job. And remember, satan asked for permission to sift Peter and the other apostles like wheat. In both cases, God gave the permission.

Satan does have power over his kingdom of darkness and in the world. First John 5:19 tells us plainly, "We know that we are of God, and that the whole world is under the power of the evil one" (BSB). Satan is the prince of the power of the air (see Eph. 2:2). Second Corinthians 4:4 calls him the god of this world, and in John 14:30 Jesus calls satan the ruler of this world. But when Christ died and was resurrected, Jesus judged the ruler of the world (see John 16:11). He disarmed the principalities and powers through His triumph on the cross (see Col. 2:15).

We have authority over the enemy in Christ. And we can take authority over prophetic witchcraft because of Christ. After the seventy disciples returned from their first mission, they were astonished that the demons were subject to them in the name of Jesus. Jesus was quick to refocus them on the big picture:

> *And He said to them, "I saw Satan fall like lightning from heaven. Behold, I give you the authority to trample on serpents and scorpions, and over all the power of the enemy, and nothing shall by any means hurt you. Nevertheless do not rejoice in this, that the spirits are subject to you, but rather rejoice because your names are written in heaven"* (Luke 10:18-20).

No one who operates in an illegitimate authority rooted in satan's kingdom has a portion in heaven. But we'll go deeper into that later in this chapter. For now, let's concentrate on satan's illegitimate authority. Jesus Himself stated, "All authority has been given to Me in heaven and on earth" (Matt. 28:18). Paul tells us Jesus is seated at the right hand of the Father in heavenly realms, "Far above all principality and power and might and dominion, and every name that is named, not only in this age but also in that which is to come" (Eph. 1:21).

We know that God exalted Jesus and gave Him "the name which is above every name, that at the name of Jesus every knee should bow, of those in heaven, and of those on earth, and of those under the earth, and that every tongue should confess that Jesus Christ is Lord, to the glory of God the Father" (Phil. 2:9-11). Jesus gave us authority over the kingdom of darkness in this powerful name, but some are misusing and abusing that name by connecting it to prophetic witchcraft.

THE FOUNDATION OF SATAN'S KINGDOM

We see opposing kingdoms in the earth. God's throne is built on the foundation of justice and righteousness (see Ps. 89:14). Satan also has a throne, but it's built on witchcraft and idolatry. Satan idolized his own beauty and wanted to be like God—and even above God. The Lord told Ezekiel all about satan's pride and his fall in Ezekiel 28:12-19:

> *You were the seal of perfection, full of wisdom and perfect in beauty. You were in Eden, the garden of God; every precious stone was your covering: the sardius, topaz, and diamond, beryl, onyx, and jasper, sapphire, turquoise, and emerald with gold. The workmanship of your timbrels and pipes was prepared for you on the day you were created.*
>
> *You were the anointed cherub who covers; I established you; you were on the holy mountain of God; you walked back and forth in the midst of fiery stones. You were perfect in your ways from the day you were created, till iniquity was found in you. By the abundance of your trading you became filled with violence within, and you sinned; therefore I cast you as a profane thing out of the mountain of God; and I destroyed you, O covering cherub, from the midst of the fiery stones.*
>
> *Your heart was lifted up because of your beauty; you corrupted your wisdom for the sake of your splendor; I cast you to the ground, I laid you before kings, that they might gaze at you. You defiled your sanctuaries by the multitude of your iniquities, by the iniquity of your trading; therefore I brought fire from your midst; it devoured you, and I turned you to ashes upon the earth in the sight of all who saw you. All who knew*

you among the peoples are astonished at you; you have become a horror, and shall be no more forever.

Isaiah 14:12-14 confirms the insight:

How you have fallen from heaven, you star of the morning, son of the dawn! You have been cut down to the earth, you who defeated the nations! But you said in your heart, "I will ascend to heaven; I will raise my throne above the stars of God, and I will sit on the mount of assembly in the recesses of the north. I will ascend above the heights of the clouds; I will make myself like the Most High" (NASB).

Lucifer decided to exalt himself above God, which is self-idolatry and rebellion, which is witchcraft. Lucifer was cast out of heaven because he wanted the throne, the authority, and the worship that belonged to God and God alone. Revelation 12:7-9 chronicles the battle:

And war broke out in heaven: Michael and his angels fought with the dragon; and the dragon and his angels fought, but they did not prevail, nor was a place found for them in heaven any longer. So the great dragon was cast out, that serpent of old, called the Devil and Satan, who deceives the whole world; he was cast to the earth, and his angels were cast out with him.

SAUL'S PROPHETIC WITCHCRAFT

Saul once respected the prophetic. The prophet Samuel anointed Saul as the first ever king of Israel, to represent God's covenant in the earth among the nations. Samuel also prophesied to Saul about a heart change. On his way back home, just as Samuel had prophesied, Saul ran into a company of prophets. First Samuel 10:10-11 describes the encounter:

> *When they came there to the hill, behold, a group of prophets met him; and the Spirit of God rushed upon him, so that he prophesied among them. And it came about, when all who previously knew him saw that he was indeed prophesying with the prophets, that the people said to one another, "What is this that has happened to the son of Kish? Is Saul also among the prophets?"* (NASB)

Saul respected the prophetic and even moved in the prophetic. He experienced the true prophetic. But he had issues. He had more fear of man than the fear of the Lord. Samuel prophesied a war assignment to Saul: go and attack Amalek and destroy everyone and everything. Saul demonstrated partial obedience, which is disobedience, by leaving King Agag alive and keeping the best of the cattle. God looked down from heaven and regretted making Saul king.

A king who was once humble got haughty. He first moved in rebellion, then into idolatry. While Samuel was on his way to rebuke Saul, the king went to Carmel to set up a monument for himself. Think about it for a minute. That is the ultimate form of self-idolatry. He didn't commission it after his death; he set up a monument to himself while he was still alive and in the midst of his rebellion. Saul no longer represented the Kingdom of light but started operating in the kingdom of darkness.

At Samuel's rebuke, Saul continued to stubbornly protest his innocence. Samuel said, "For rebellion is as the sin of witchcraft. and stubbornness is as iniquity and idolatry. Because you have rejected the word of the Lord, He also has rejected you from being king" (1 Sam.

15:23). Only then did Saul repent, but his he already lost his anointing. An evil spirit came to torment him. He started trying to kill David, and ultimately he died after consulting the witch at Endor because he could not hear from the Lord. A man who once valued the prophetic died after visiting a diviner. What a sad ending.

JEZEBEL'S PROPHETIC WITCHCRAFT

Jezebel also operated in prophetic witchcraft. The Old Testament Queen Jezebel and the New Testament false prophetess Jezebel were both immoral idolaters. In the Old Testament, the wicked queen sought to cut off the prophetic voice, even releasing a prophetic witchcraft death curse against Elijah. In the New Testament, the woman Jezebel was teaching false doctrine.

What many haven't understood is the spirit of Jezebel existed long before either of these women who carried the characteristics of the demon they served. The spirit of Jezebel influenced both these women to operate in false prophetic maneuvers. God used Elijah to prophesy the demise of the wicked queen, and Jesus Himself told of the fate of that woman Jezebel. He spoke to the church at Thyatira, which by the way was the same city in which the girl with the spirit of divination lived.

> *I know your works, love, service, faith, and your patience; and as for your works, the last are more than the first. Nevertheless I have a few things against you, because you allow that woman Jezebel, who calls herself a prophetess, to teach and seduce My servants to commit sexual immorality and eat things sacrificed to idols.*

And I gave her time to repent of her sexual immorality, and she did not repent. Indeed I will cast her into a sickbed, and those who commit adultery with her into great tribulation, unless they repent of their deeds. I will kill her children with death, and all the churches shall know that I am He who searches the minds and hearts. And I will give to each one of you according to your works (Revelation 2:19-23).

This is how much Jesus hates prophetic witchcraft. The good news is there are rewards to those who overcome prophetic witchcraft's lure. There are rewards to those who don't bow down, cave in, or tolerate prophetic witchcraft, which comes from the depths of satan's kingdom. Jesus explains in Revelation 2:24-28:

Now to you I say, and to the rest in Thyatira, as many as do not have this doctrine, who have not known the depths of Satan, as they say, I will put on you no other burden. But hold fast what you have till I come. And he who overcomes, and keeps My works until the end, to him I will give power over the nations—"He shall rule them with a rod of iron; they shall be dashed to pieces like the potter's vessels"—as I also have received from My Father; and I will give him the morning star.

WHY FALSE PROPHETS ARE GOING TO HELL

False prophets will go to hell. So it's important to understand what a false prophet is and refuse to come into agreement with false prophetic operations, which lead us into deception. Jesus warned us about false prophets in Matthew 7:15: "Beware of false prophets, who come to you in sheep's clothing, but inwardly they are ravenous wolves."

The Passion Translation puts a new light on this oft-quoted verse: "Constantly be on your guard against phony prophets. They come disguised as lambs, appearing to be genuine, but on the inside they are like wild, ravenous wolves!" And *The Message* says, "Be wary of false preachers who smile a lot, dripping with practiced sincerity. Chances are they are out to rip you off some way or other."

It's important to remember what a false prophet is. A false prophet is not one who misses it or one who makes poor judgment calls in ministry operations as they learn and grow. No, a false prophet, in the simplest terms, is one who sets out to deceive. The motive is to gain something to consume upon their own lusts outside the will of God, whether that's money, fame, or some other reward. They don't seek God for what they need, but rather they manipulate their way into what they want.

Jesus gave us a second warning about false prophets in the end times in Matthew 24:11: "Then many false prophets will rise up and deceive many." Notice the double use of the word *many*. It doesn't say "a few false prophets will rise up and deceive unbelievers." It doesn't say "many false prophets will rise up and deceive a few." It paints a picture of a vast number of false prophets deceiving a vast number of people. In fact, the Greek word for *many* in that verse is *polus*. *HELPS Word Studies* defines it as "many (high in number); multitudinous, plenteous, much, great in amount (extent)."

Again, false prophets are going to hell. Revelation 21:8 makes that very clear: "But the cowardly, unbelieving, abominable, murderers, sexually immoral, sorcerers, idolaters, and all liars shall have their part in the lake which burns with fire and brimstone, which is the second death." False prophets are operating in the kingdom of darkness, often making money or fame their idol and lying about prophetic words, visions, dreams, and encounters.

False prophets are falsely representing God's Kingdom and operating from a place of idolatry and witchcraft, purporting to speak in the name of Jesus without any true relationship with Him. Jesus said in Matthew 7:21-23:

> *Not everyone who says to Me, "Lord, Lord," shall enter the kingdom of heaven, but he who does the will of My Father in heaven. Many will say to Me in that day, "Lord, Lord, have we not prophesied in Your name, cast out demons in Your name, and done many wonders in Your name?" And then I will declare to them, "I never knew you; depart from Me, you who practice lawlessness!"*

False prophets and prophetic people are speaking false words with an illegitimate authority. When Jesus ascended to the Father, He gave gifts to men—apostles, prophets, evangelists, pastors, and teachers (see Eph. 4:11). God did not give false prophets to the church. Satan did. I have said many times, I don't believe false prophets start out as false prophets, if they were ever prophets at all. Rather, they are tempted, as James says:

> *Let no one say when he is tempted, "I am tempted by God"; for God cannot be tempted by evil, nor does He Himself tempt anyone. But each one is tempted when he is drawn away by his own desires and enticed. Then, when desire has conceived, it gives birth to sin; and sin, when it is full-grown, brings forth death* (James 1:13-15).

Jesus never knew them. They weren't serving Jesus, who said, "No one can serve two masters; for either he will hate the one and love the other, or else he will be loyal to the one and despise the other. You cannot serve God and mammon" (Matt. 6:24). Prophetic witchcraft does not glorify God; it glorifies the enemy, and those who operate in it are not worshiping God but idols. False prophets are serving another kingdom. Paul put it this way, "But evil men and impostors will grow worse and worse, deceiving and being deceived" (2 Tim. 3:13).

NOTE

1. "Snake owner Daniel Brandon killed by his pet python," BBC News, January 24, 2018, https://www.bbc.com/news/uk-england -hampshire-42801983.

CHAPTER 7

EXPOSING SCRIPTURE
TWISTING

*T*ouch not my anointed and do my prophets no harm. The Holy Spirit inspired Bible writers to pen these words in First Chronicles 16:22 and Psalm 105:15. These are the first verses you'll hear if you question a false prophet's twisted theology.

Unfortunately, since the restoration of the prophetic movement we've seen this verse misused and abused as a weapon to manipulate the saints. Yes, these Scriptures are in the Bible, but Scripture twisters use it as a force field against accountability. These verses are used to make the false prophet untouchable, unchallengeable. These verses make idols out of mere men.

False prophets use these verses as a shield to deflect your disagreement. Controlling prophets use these verses to force you into submission. Cultish prophets uses these verses to shame you if you don't see eye to eye with the spiritually abusive rules of the congregation. Jezebel's prophets and yes-men bodyguards will even threaten and curse you for crossing the line of these Scriptures, which are being taken out of context.

When God inspired David to write Psalm 105:15, it wasn't an isolated verse He intended to weaponize. Looking at the context of verse 15 helps us understand that God wasn't elevating prophets to untouchable status. We're all God's anointed ones, as we have an anointing that abides in us (see 1 John 2:27). Christ is the Anointed One, and as Christians we are little anointed ones. You may not be a prophet, but you have Christ's anointing in you.

LEVIATHAN INFLUENCING SCRIPTURE TWISTERS

The Leviathan spirit is a twisting spirit. I believe this is one of the principalities inspiring some of the Scripture twisting we're seeing in the Body of Christ—and even outside the Body of Christ.

According to *Eastman's Bible Dictionary*, *leviathan* is a transliterated Hebrew word (*livyathan*) meaning "twisted, coiled." The dictionary reveals, "In Job 3:8, Revised Version, and marg. of Authorized Version, it denotes the dragon which, according to Eastern tradition, is an enemy of light."

Think about it for a minute. If the entrance of God's Word brings light (see Ps. 119:130) then the entrance of error brings darkness. As I wrote in my book *The Spiritual Warrior's Guide to Defeating Water Spirits*, "Leviathan's reasoning can seem beautiful in the mind of the one it deceives. Leviathan's lies makes its victim feel strong and courageous against opponents, which is a manifestation of pride. ...Leviathan's words will burn you and his smoke will cloud your vision and bring confusion."

God used Leviathan—a real rather than some mythological creature—in His discussion with Job to reveal to us how this spirit operates. It has more than one head. It twists words. It brings mourning. It's patient, waiting for an opportunity to strike. It tries to drown its victims.

The Bible makes stark warning about changing the Word of God—and twisting Scripture qualifies. Proverbs 30:5-6 warns, "Every word of God is pure; He is a shield to those who put their trust in Him. Do not add to His words, lest He rebuke you, and you be found a liar." In Deuteronomy 4:2, God insists, "You shall not add to the word which I command you, nor take from it, that you may keep the commandments of the Lord your God which I command you."

TARGETING THE VULNERABLE WITH TWISTED TRUTH

While there are legitimate differences in interpretation of Scripture—some believe the gifts of the Spirit are no longer for today and some believe various end-time theologies—honest differences in understanding Scripture are not the same as twisting Scripture for one's own benefit. Twisted Scripture is usually birthed from wrong motives, such as greed, and used to support the false prophet's perspectives.

Scripture twisters have been roaming the earth since the early church days. Peter sternly warned against false teachers in Second Peter 2:1: "But there were also false prophets among the people, even as there will be false teachers among you, who will secretly bring in destructive heresies, even denying the Lord who bought them, and bring on themselves swift destruction." Peter explains that Scripture twisters are clever and advance evil teaching and shameful immorality. What's more, they slander the truth. And Second Peter 2:3 tells us why: "In their greed they will make up clever lies to get hold of your money" (NLT).

Paul echoed Peter's warning in Acts 20:30, "Also from among your-selves men will rise up, speaking perverse things, to draw away the disciples after themselves." And Peter understood false prophets and teachers in his era were twisting Paul's words: "Some of his comments are hard to understand, and those who are ignorant and unstable have twisted his letters to mean something quite different, just as they do with other parts of Scripture. And this will result in their destruction" (2 Pet. 3:16 NLT). Of course, false ones don't just twist Paul's words, they will twist any Scriptures that forward their wrong motive, which, again, is usually money.

Catch this. *Strebloo*, the Greek word for "twist" in Second Peter 3:16, carries the connotation of torture. According to *The KJV New Testament Greek Lexicon*, *strebloo* means "twist, turn awry, to torture, put to the rack," and is a metaphor for "pervert, of one who wrests or tortures language in a false sense." The Scripture twister is perverting the pure Word of God. Those who twist Scripture are, in effect, torturing the souls of unbelievers and violently forcing them to pervert their faith.

Scripture twisters target those who do not know the Word or are so desperate for a breakthrough they are willing to set aside accurate the-ology for the false promises the prophets preach. Peter said they "entice unstable souls" (see 2 Pet. 2:14). And he told Timothy, "This sort are those who creep into households and make captives of gullible women loaded down with sins, led away by various lusts, always learning and never able to come to the knowledge of the truth" (2 Tim. 3:5-7).

MEGA MONEY MAGNETS

The money prophets—renamed by some in the current days as CashApp prophets because they go live on Facebook multiple times a day with a headline, "Can I prophesy?"—are all about the money. While ministry costs money and it's appropriate to sow at church and conferences as led by the Lord, the money prophets manipulate for greenbacks.

Don't get me wrong. I believe God can miraculously provide money. I remember once I was in North Florida, stuck in the dark after my car broke down. I was broke, busted, and disgusted, as they say, with only a few pennies in my bank account and a few dollars in my purse. I didn't know what to do, so I prayed. When I looked through my purse again, I found a crisp, clean $100 bill that paved the way for me to stay indoors that night and eat breakfast the next day. I've also seen supernatural debt cancellation in my ministry.

Again, there's nothing wrong with taking up an offering or even challenging people to give, but when people make promises God won't keep, when they emphasize money miracles as an earmark of their ministry, and when they pressure people to give, there's rotten fruit. It's called the love of money, which is a root of all kinds of evil (see 1 Tim. 6:10). The Bible says you cannot serve both God and mammon (see Matt. 6:24). Sadly, many preachers and prophets are serving mammon.

I once received an e-mail from a false prophet that exaggerates my point, but this goes to show you what's out there (in case you haven't seen it):

> This morning, as I was in my prayer chambers meditating on the Word of the Lord for you and countless others, the Lord screamed a mighty scream in the form of a strong wind blowing from the north and commanded me to look up from which cometh my help.
>
> The Spirit revealed to me a little mistake that I was making. While I have been running around left and right

trying to balance my financial challenges, I momentarily forgot the reason the Lord has placed me in a season of famine. With over $100,000 in financial endeavors, I have been holding on to your breakthrough by keeping this a secret from you. You see, when a prophet is in a season of famine, God is looking to release to those who would lift him out of the famine, a miracle of breakthrough.

As your personal prophet, it is unlawful for me to hold onto your breakthrough! Precious one, this one little mistake has already cost me over $100,000 but I will not allow it to cost you your breakthrough. God has commanded me to ask every faithful partner who's ready for a miraculous breakthrough to help lift this financial boulder off the shoulders of the prophet with a powerful donation of faith in the amounts of either $300 or $1000.

If you stand with me with the $397 donation, I will send you an MP3 or CD (CD upon request) with the company of prophets and myself speaking a word of breakthrough into your situation for the next twelve months. Beloved of God, I need your support in this season ... I will lift up mine eyes unto the hills, from whence cometh my help. My help cometh from the LORD, which made heaven and earth (Psalms 121:1-2).

Paul speaks of those who are "teaching things which they ought not, for the sake of dishonest gain" (Tit. 1:11). Jude laments, "Woe to them! For they have gone in the way of Cain, have run greedily in the error of Balaam for profit, and perished in the rebellion of Korah" (Jude 11). And again, "These are grumblers, complainers, walking according to their own lusts; and they mouth great swelling words, flattering people to gain advantage" (Jude 16).

THE SAMUEL DECEPTION

A recent heretical assumption in the prophetic movement is what I call the Samuel Deception. It's rooted in First Samuel 3:19-20, "So Samuel grew, and the Lord was with him and let none of his words fall to the ground. And all Israel from Dan to Beersheba knew that Samuel had been established as a prophet of the Lord."

It was clear that Samuel indeed carried a stellar reputation throughout the land. When Saul and his servant went out to look for his father's donkeys, they had no success. After days, the servant was inspired by God with an idea on how to solve the problem: "I've just thought of something! There is a man of God who lives here in this town. He is held in high honor by all the people because everything he says comes true. Let's go find him. Perhaps he can tell us which way to go" (1 Sam. 9:6 NLT). The servant was right. Samuel knew exactly where the donkeys were.

Some aggressive prophets will insist that they can never miss it. Any prophet who insists they are not capable of missing it has already missed it. New Testament prophecy is fallible, and missing the mark with a prophetic word is not the sign of a false prophet. I talk about the signs of a false prophet in my book *Discerning Prophetic Witchcraft*.

But beyond that, this heresy suggests that God is responsible to back up what the prophet prophesies, even if what they said did not originate in God's heart. This puts God at man's service, as if the Almighty is actually a wizard behind a curtain or a genie in a bottle. This puts

God at our command rather than putting us at His command. And the twisting of First Samuel 3:19 is gaining momentum.

HYPER-GRACE SANCTIONS SIN

Thank God for His grace. The grace of God empowers me and has transformed my life—and is transforming my life. His grace is sufficient for any trial, temptation, or battle we face. But there's a dangerous error called hyper-grace that is proliferating in the Body of Christ like a cancer. Hyper-grace messengers tell you our past, present, and future sins have already been forgiven so repentance is no longer necessary for the born-again believer.

We know that's an error, for if it were true the Holy Spirit would not convict of us sin. We would not have to confess our sins one to another so we can be healed (see James 5:14-15). If that were true, Paul would not have disciplined believers in Corinth because of their sin (see 1 Cor. 11:27-32). If we don't have to repent, why did Jesus have something against some of the churches He spoke to in the Book of Revelation?

Hyper-grace is not just stretching the truth, it's a distortion of truth that leads people into grave error. I received a message once from a man named Roy who was in absolute anguish. He wrote:

> I'm in desperate need of advice. I recently disassociated with the hypergrace movement and it has left me in a spiritual struggle, from anxiety and depression to straight up confusion and other mental symptoms. Unbelief has eroded me pretty well. I have questioned my salvation and even God's existence and I can barely even read the Word without being critical and doubtful. Have I crossed

the unforgivable line? Is there still hope for me? This has been going on about 4 months. I feel as if my heart has hardened. I really want my sincerity for God and spiritual things to return! Thanks for any help.

What a heartbreaking testimony! You can hear the desperation. You can see the struggle. I understand all too well how disassociating with a movement the Holy Spirit shows you is riddled with errors and extremes can cause a faith crisis. I've been there with the extreme apostolic movement that values building one's own personal kingdom before family—and ultimately even God.

PUTTING PROPHECY ON PAR WITH SCRIPTURE

Prophecy is not on par with Scripture. Let me say that again. Prophecy is not on par with Scripture. Some prophets and preachers insist their words carry the weight and authority of the inspired canon, but this is an error. While cessationists who believe the gifts of God are not for today are also in error, the argument that prophetic revelations are Scripture-quality is perhaps a more dangerous error in the end.

The error that prophecy is on par with Scripture is hardly new. It can be traced all the way back to Montanism. This early Christian movement that started in the late second century A.D. was also called New Prophecy and is now also known as the Cataphrygian heresy. A prophet named Montanus, who came out of the church in Phrygia in Asia Minor, spread the deception that continued strong through the ninth century.

"He fell into a trance and began to 'prophesy under the influence of the Spirit.' He was soon joined by two young women, Prisca, or Priscilla, and Maximilla, who also began to prophesy. The movement spread throughout Asia Minor. Inscriptions have indicated that a number of towns were almost completely converted to Montanism," according to Britannica.com.

> The essential principle of Montanism was that the Paraclete, the Spirit of truth, whom Jesus had promised in the Gospel According to John, was manifesting himself to the world through Montanus and the prophets and prophetesses associated with him. This did not seem at first to deny the doctrines of the church or to attack the authority of the bishops. Prophecy from the earliest days had been held in honour, and the church acknowledged the charismatic gift of some prophets.

> It soon became clear, however, that the Montanist prophecy was new. True prophets did not, as Montanus did, deliberately induce a kind of ecstatic intensity and a state of passivity and then maintain that the words they spoke were the voice of the Spirit. It also became clear that the claim of Montanus to have the final revelation of the Holy Spirit implied that something could be added to the teaching of Christ and the Apostles and that, therefore, the church had to accept a fuller revelation.

While the movement ended over one thousand years ago, the seed of this heresy is taking root in the modern-day prophetic movement. While God reveals present truth and prophecies that come from God's heart are His words, that does not mean a prophet can demand obedience to his prophecies. Paul told us not to despise prophecy, to examine all things, and to hold fast to that which is good for a reason (see 1 Thess. 5:20-21).

WHEN LOYALTY BECOMES LETHAL

Loyalty is admirable until it becomes lethal. False prophets and those operating in prophetic witchcraft love to play the loyalty card. Unconditional loyalty that's demanded is toxic and equals spiritual abuse. The problem with unconditional loyalty from a big picture perspective is that it leads to cover-ups of sinful behavior among leadership. The sin always finds the leader out, and those who covered it up are left broken and disillusioned.

Again, loyalty is an admirable quality, but when it's demanded, it can become perverted. Like love, loyalty believes the best, but when loyalty sees the worst it doesn't turn a blind eye. Toxic loyalty works to protect the leader at all costs, even when the leader is bringing harm to people and shame to the name of Jesus behind the scenes. Justice trumps loyalty.

Godly loyalty is reciprocated. Toxic loyalty only runs one way. Ultimately, our only unconditional loyalty belongs to God. God is unconditionally loyal to us. He will never leave us or forsake us. He is faithful even when we are unfaithful (see 2 Tim. 2:13). If your loyalty to a person is greater than your loyalty to God and His Word, it's toxic and will poison your relationships.

DISCERNING SCRIPTURE TWISTING

Scripture twisting isn't always so blatant. In fact, it's subtle. Remember the snake in the garden was more subtle than any other creature. Satan twisted God's words and is still inspiring people to do the same. If it were always obvious, we wouldn't need discernment. Throughout the pages of Scripture, we're warned about false operations so that we won't take everything we hear as gospel truth.

Jesus said, "Beloved, do not believe every spirit, but test the spirits, whether they are of God; because many false prophets have gone out into the world" (1 John 4:1). That doesn't apply only to prophetic words, but to teaching the Word as well. And Peter wrote, "You therefore, beloved, since you know this beforehand, beware lest you also fall from your own steadfastness, being led away with the error of the wicked; but grow in the grace and knowledge of our Lord and Savior Jesus Christ" (2 Pet. 3:17-18).

Be a Good Berean

Your primary best defense against Scripture twisters is to be what I call a good Berean. The Book of Acts gives us a hint into their character. Paul was preaching the gospel of Jesus Christ and it was falling on the ears of Jews and Gentiles alike. Acts 17:11 tells us, "And the people of Berea were more open-minded than those in Thessalonica, and they listened eagerly to Paul's message. They searched the Scriptures day after day to see if Paul and Silas were teaching the truth" (NLT).

As I wrote in *The Prophet's Devotional*, "The Bereans were first open-minded. They wanted to learn new things. They didn't camp out in the last move of God, set in their ways and rejecting present-day truth. They were hungering and thirsting after righteousness, and were continually filled."

We all need to embrace a Berean spirit. The Bereans were biblically curious. The Bereans didn't just read the Scriptures, they searched the Scriptures. The Bereans didn't just search the Scriptures randomly; they were searching with the intent of confirming truth. Put another way, they were lovers of the truth and able to rightly divide the word of truth (see 2 Tim. 2:15). They were students of the Word.

The English Standard Version of Acts 17:11 says they examined the Scriptures daily. They examined the Scriptures so they could hold fast to that which is good (see 1 Thess. 5:21). They set out to discern whether what they heard matched up with what God had already said. They were judging a righteous judgment (see John 7:24).

The Bereans had noble character and were fair-minded. The International Standard Version calls them receptive. They were intelligent, open to conviction, teachable, and less biased than the rest. They were diligent, searching the Scriptures daily.

Before Paul wrote Second Timothy 3:16-17, the Bereans embraced it: "All Scripture is inspired by God and is useful to teach us what is true and to make us realize what is wrong in our lives. It corrects us when we are wrong and teaches us to do what is right. God uses it to prepare and equip his people to do every good work" (NLT).

You can't depend on your pastor's Sunday message alone to renew your mind to the truth. We all need to study to show ourselves approved, so we can rightly divide the word of truth (see 2 Tim. 2:15).

Pursue Intimacy with God

Cultivating the oil of intimacy in our lives requires time in God's presence, as well as renewing our minds with Scriptures about who we are in Christ and His love for us. We must have faith and confidence in our position in Him. When we know who we are and can hear His voice, we'll be less likely to fall for the Scripture-twisting tactics of false prophets.

We gain intimacy with God by studying His emotions; through praising, worshiping, and fellowshipping with Him; and by determining to seek, obey, and please Him in our thoughts, words, and deeds. When we seek to abide in Him, we are cultivating the oil of intimacy. When we draw near to God, He promises to draw near to us (see James 4:8).

Cultivate Spiritual Growth

Spiritual growth is a lifetime quest. We will never stop growing. Even through eternity we will continue learning of God. Peter lays out a spiritual growth plan, which will guard you from Scripture twisters, in Second Peter 1:5-10:

> *But also for this very reason, giving all diligence, add to your faith virtue, to virtue knowledge, to knowledge self-control, to self-control perseverance, to perseverance godliness, to godliness brotherly kindness, and to brotherly kindness love. For if these things are yours and abound, you will be neither barren nor unfruitful in the knowledge of our Lord Jesus Christ. For he who lacks these things is shortsighted, even to blindness, and has forgotten that he was cleansed from his old sins. Therefore, brethren, be even more diligent to make your call and election sure, for if you do these things you will never stumble.*

If you have fallen for Scripture-twisting tactics—or been involved in doing this yourself—repent. God is slow to anger and abounding in mercy.

CHAPTER 8

SIGNS YOU ARE UNDER A PROPHETIC WITCHCRAFT ATTACK

Just months before I resigned as editor of *Charisma* magazine—one of the biggest career transitions in my life—I fell deathly ill. The day after I came home from taping television episodes on *The Jim Bakker Show*, my body completely shut down. I wasn't just exhausted, I was unknowingly battling a spirit of death based on a witchcraft curse of which I was unaware.

I still have vivid memories of being unable to get up out of bed. If I did get out of bed, I could work two or maybe three hours and had to go back to bed. I could not muster the strength to exercise. I developed a stutter for several months. After six months of this and trying everything in my power to break hexes, vexes, incantations, potions, spells, and witchcraft, I was at my wits' end. Anxiety started flooding my soul as I thought this was my new normal. I saw my dreams going down the drain.

Of course, I went to doctors—and they could find no official medical diagnosis. They gave me herbs and elixirs and suggested lots of sleep and a low-carb diet. None of that helped. I was frustrated, but continued as best I could to push through. By the grace of God I maintained my ministry, finished book deadlines, and ministered at church on Sundays. But it was completely the grace of God and when the anointing lifted, I would be almost debilitated.

This lasted for the better part of two years. Then one January, the Lord told me when I went to Europe in June I would be free from this plague. I thought to myself, *But that's six months from now!* It didn't make sense to my mind, but I couldn't see what was coming against me. Again, I was binding, loosing, pushing back darkness. I was doing everything a noble spiritual warrior would do and had others praying. I would get short reprieves during which I felt normal, but the ailments always came back.

When I went to Europe in June, I was very ill. Day by day passed and I was waiting for the Lord to break this curse to no avail. Every day, I felt weaker and weaker. On the day before I was to head back to the United States, I woke up with the migraine of migraines. It was not a normal headache and I had never experienced anything like it before. I was in such agony, I literally felt like pulling my hair out of my head. No aspirin or anything else took the pain away.

Then finally, out of nowhere, 12 hours later, the pain left. At that time, I got a phone call from my host saying there was a prophet there who wanted to pray for me before she left. I instinctively knew this was the moment of breakthrough and bounded down three flights of stairs to the conference center. There the prophet started praying and literally saw little minion cursing demons surrounding me. She said, "I wouldn't be surprised if you were having symptoms in your physical body."

This prophet had no idea what I had been walking through but she saw the curses and took authority over them. She had details on the origination of the curses, which came from a surprising source, and with that exposure the curse broke. When I went home, I was completely free of any symptoms. I felt and looked fifteen years younger. In fact, people flat-out asked me what I did to look so good. Praise God.

Witchcraft attacks come against our mind and body. The first step to overcoming them is to discern witchcraft is operating. Sometimes, you need someone to help you break it, especially when the hordes of hell have been unleashed against you. One can put a thousand to flight and two can put ten thousand to flight (see Josh. 23:10). As I always say, an enemy exposed is an enemy defeated. The prophet in Europe exposed not just the witchcraft but the source of it, thereby allowing us to cut it off at the root.

EXPOSING PROPHETIC WITCHCRAFT ATTACKS

The Merriam-Webster Dictionary defines *witchcraft* as an irresistible influence or fascination—and the Bible warns us not to be bewitched: "You crazy Galatians! Did someone put a spell on you? Have you taken leave of your senses? Something crazy has happened, for it's obvious that you no longer have the crucified Jesus in clear focus in your lives" (Gal. 3:1 MSG).

Obviously, there is a spiritual force that the Bible is warning us about. It causes us to take leave of our senses. Witchcraft releases strong confusion against our minds so that Jesus is not the clear focus of our lives. Once that happens, we are more vulnerable to the vain imaginations the enemy whispers to our souls. We have a responsibility to know about this spiritual wickedness and guard ourselves against it.

When you are aware of how prophetic witchcraft attacks, you can expose it with the light of God's Word and break its powers. Principalities release the power of witchcraft. Just as the power of God—the Holy Spirit—heals and delivers, the power of the enemy—witchcraft—brings on sickness and otherwise oppresses.

Let's look at some of the symptoms of a prophetic witchcraft attack. Keep in mind, all of these symptoms may not apply, and some of these symptoms could be due to other issues in your life. The key is to gain awareness of how prophetic witchcraft attacks so you can more easily discern it and break it.

You feel like you are being watched.

When you are under a prophetic witchcraft attack, you may feel like you are being watched. I've experienced this many times and it's an eerie, uncomfortable feeling. I later learned it was because monitoring spirits had been assigned to me. The girl with the spirit of divination in Acts 16 was clearly watching—and following—Paul and Silas. As its name suggests, a monitoring spirit is a spirit that monitors you.

Monitoring spirits work in the realm of witchcraft. They are spiritual peeping toms and evil eavesdroppers. They are satanic watchdogs. They are illegal informants. They are part of a demonic network that watches and reports information back to higher ranking demonic powers so they can devise plans to steal, kill, and destroy you.

Monitoring spirits are like the devil's private investigators. You can't see them, but they can see and hear you. The devil is not omnipresent or omniscient, so he depends on monitoring spirits to gather information. Other names for monitoring spirits are familiar spirits, masquerading spirits, ancestral spirits, fowlers, besiegers, spirit spies, demonic messengers, and watchers. I teach more about this in my School of the Seers.

You start dropping things or get clumsy.

If you find you suddenly have butterfingers, it could be witchcraft is attacking you. If you are not usually clumsy, but suddenly start dropping your phone, tripping over things, or generally have poor motor skills it could be the sign of prophetic witchcraft or even a prophetic curse. It may seem almost like the object leaped out of your hand while you're fumbling to grasp it.

You lose your motivation.

I'm an extremely motivated person, so I know when I lose all motivation and just want to blow everything off, it's likely witchcraft. Loss of motivation is a sure sign of prophetic witchcraft because witchcraft demotivates and demoralizes you. If you are usually a responsible person who stays on top of your tasks, but find that you are suddenly putting things off until tomorrow that should be done today because you just don't feel like doing it, you could be under a prophetic witchcraft spell that's trying to bring you into poverty. Proverbs 10:4 assures, "Lazy people are soon poor; hard workers get rich" (NLT).

You can't hear from God.

When prophetic witchcraft attacks, you may feel like your mind is a scrambled egg. You can't concentrate on the Word and you are having a hard time hearing the voice of God, if you can hear Him at all. Prophetic witchcraft makes it harder to hear God because your mind is cloudy and your brain is foggy. You become dull of hearing.

You are hearing voices.

Prophetic witchcraft is intent on you not hearing from the Lord yourself so you will be dependent on false prophetic voices instead. Demons don't have bodies, but they have voices. Perhaps the enemy is threatening you, or perhaps it's a voice discouraging you. Prophetic witchcraft has a voice that seeks to derail God's plan for your life and leave you desperate enough to turn to outside sources for clarity.

You have evil forebodings.

Perhaps you are suddenly fearful or even paranoid. This is the realm of evil forebodings. Proverbs 15:15 says, "All the days of the desponding and afflicted are made evil [by anxious thoughts and forebodings], but he who has a glad heart has a continual feast [regardless of circumstances]" (AMPC).

These evil forebodings then bring a ripple effect of behaviors. You may feel like everyone is out to get you and you can't trust anyone around you. You may tap into conspiracy-like theories about what people around you are doing or hiding from you. You may start abruptly withdrawing from people to protect yourself.

You have a death wish.

When Jezebel's witchcraft-laced curse hit Elijah, he ran for his life and wished he was dead.

This type of sudden death wish is associated with prophetic witchcraft and curses. If you are on the mountaintop one day and feel like you are in the Valley of the Shadow of Death the next day, it's likely prophetic witchcraft has attacked your mind.

Your emotions are out of whack.

Perhaps you are generally an agreeable person, but you find yourself irritable, angry, and frustrated. You may feel depressed or anxious. You are on an emotional rollercoaster out of the blue. You may feel like people and things are standing in your way. You may get mad at yourself, mad at the devil, or even mad at God. You may feel oppressed, like you are carrying a heavy emotional burden.

You are making mountains out of molehills.

Prophetic witchcraft turns little things into massive issues. You get anxious and start catastrophizing events in your life. You're sick and tired of your circumstances, but what you don't realize is that the enemy is magnifying your circumstances with distorted mirrors and smoke that clouds reality.

You feel confused.

Prophetic witchcraft makes you question yourself, question your friends—question God. When witchcraft attacks, it's difficult to make sound decisions. When strong confusion hits your mind, you can be sure it's not coming from God. God is not the author of confusion but of peace (see 1 Cor. 14:33).

Prophetic witchcraft can make you confused about your life. You don't know why you got so many prophecies that haven't come to pass. You make decisions based on what you think God's will is but you have a wrong understanding of God's will because you bought into the lies of prophetic witchcraft.

Remember, confusion is part of the curse of the law: "The Lord will send on you cursing, confusion, and rebuke in all that you set your hand

EXPOSING PROPHETIC WITCHCRAFT

to do, until you are destroyed and until you perish quickly, because of the wickedness of your doings in which you have forsaken Me" (Deut. 28:20). God isn't sending confusion on you, but your disobedience to put your trust in the words of a diviner can allow the enemy to release confusion on your life.

You are forgetful.

I once entirely forgot about a meeting in New York City. I was ready to go the night before, but by the next morning I went about my usual business. Finally, I remembered I was supposed to be in New York because a flight alert popped up on my email, but it was too late to get to the airport.

Prophetic witchcraft can make you forgetful. You may forget your keys—I've done this many times—forget birthdays, or even forget what the Word says. You may forget what you are saying mid-sentence and not be able to get your train of thought back. You may overlook obvious mistakes in your work or forget a key instruction or deadline.

You make poor financial decisions.

Prophetic witchcraft causes you to make poor financial decisions. Prophetic witchcraft can work in the realm of hype. What is hype? Hype puts on a show to stir your emotions so they rise above the spiritual senses of your spiritual discernment.

Haggai 1:6 reads: "You have sown much, but you have reaped little; you eat, but you do not have enough; you drink, but you do not have your fill; you clothe yourselves, but no one is warm; and he who earns wages has earned them to put them in a bag with holes in it" (AMPC). When you sow into prophetic witchcraft, you are not going to see a return on that investment.

You may feel stuck or like you are wandering.

Prophetic witchcraft will leave you feeling stuck and wandering. It may seem as if you are going around the same mountain over and over again, making no progress in your natural life or your spiritual life. Wandering is directly associated with prophetic witchcraft in Zechariah 10:2: "For the household gods utter nonsense, and the diviners see lies; they tell false dreams and give empty consolation. Therefore the people wander like sheep; they are afflicted for lack of a shepherd" (ESV).

You may feel like you are in a perpetual wilderness, never able to enter your proverbial Promised Land. This is a result of coming into agreement with prophetic witchcraft. Jeremiah 23:32 tells us:

> "Indeed, I am against those who prophesy false dreams," declares the Lord. "They tell them and lead my people astray with their reckless lies, yet I did not send or appoint them. They do not benefit these people in the least," declares the Lord (NIV).

You have abnormal loyalty to a prophet, church, or network.

Prophetic witchcraft will drive you to abnormal loyalty. I stayed in a Jezebelic church for two years after the Holy Spirit told me to leave because I was so loyal to the vision, had poured so much of my life into the congregation, and had so many friends there.

Prophetic witchcraft may drive you to toxic loyalty because people who tap into prophetic witchcraft seek to form soul ties with you through information seeking. You may idolize the prophet and make great sacrifices, both personally and financially, for them. It could also be that you feel intimidated to break away from the person or organization that's moving in prophetic witchcraft. Make no mistake, prophetic witchcraft will divide you from friends and family.

You forget who you really are.

You are a child of the King. You are the righteousness of God in Christ Jesus. Greater is He who is in you than he that is in the world. You are blessed coming in and blessed going out. Everything you put your hand to prospers. That's your legal position. But when prophetic witchcraft attacks, you feel like a worthless worm. You forget who you are in Christ and have little to no interest in the Word, church, praise, worship, or the like. You may feel guilt, condemnation, or self-pity. Witchcraft attacks your identity and position with God. If the devil can get you to question your own authority, you won't exercise authority over him.

Just plain worn out.

If you've slept eight hours, had a tall cup of coffee, and you still feel like you've been run over by a truck, prophetic witchcraft could be attacking you. I've learned not to give in by lying down for a nap that turns into four or five hours of witchcraft-induced sleep. If you are eating well, sleeping well, exercising well, and living well—and if you are generally healthy—you shouldn't feel like you're walking through quicksand. This could be a witchcraft attack.

People are attacking you in spurts.

When people start attacking you and making false accusations against you in droves, it's a sign the enemy is inspiring them to word-curse you and, in doing so, release witchcraft. This is not a random ill-mannered person or a single obnoxious e-mail. This is a flood of attacks, and you may begin to feel everything has turned on you.

PROPHETIC WITCHCRAFT'S NOCTURNAL ATTACKS

We're going to spend a lot of time on this one because it's a common area of attack for witchcraft. Think about it for a minute. The devil loves to work in darkness. When you are asleep, your defenses are down. You are not binding and loosing while you are tossing and turning. We're going to look at nocturnal attacks.

According to *The Seer's Dictionary*, nocturnal attacks are spiritual attacks that often come through nightmares, night visions, or sleep disturbances. We are going to look at prophetic witchcraft manifesting through insomnia, nightmares, night terrors, witchcraft-laced dreams, sleep paralysis, and lacerations on the body.

When Insomnia Strikes

Insomnia is the inability to get enough sleep or trouble falling asleep or staying asleep. Technically, one night of lost sleep doesn't equal insomnia. When prophetic witchcraft attacks, though, it can lead you into a season of insomnia if you don't break it quickly. You may fall asleep easily because you are exhausted but find yourself waking up between twelve and three in the morning unable to go back to sleep. These are the witching hours when demonic activity is at its peak.

One of the ways witchcraft keeps you up at night is through worry. The enemy brings thoughts to your mind about the problems and challenges of the season and you ruminate. That leads to anxiety and dread, which can make you too nervous to settle down. Psalm 127:2 calls this the bread of anxious toil. And Ecclesiastes 2:23 tells us the anxious have no rest for their minds at night.

Nasty Nightmares

One year, witchcraft couldn't get me by day. I was ready for the onslaught. So instead, witchcraft attacked me at night—in my sleep. I have had some of the worst nightmares in the last two weeks that I've ever had in my entire life. Things I won't even speak out loud because the power of death and life is in the tongue. Indeed, the enemy wants me to speak out the disturbing pictures he offered to give them life.

Proverbs 3:24 promises us when we lay down we will not be afraid and our sleep will be sweet. That is God's will for our lives, but prophetic witchcraft brings nightmares. Interestingly, *The Merriam-Webster Dictionary* defines *nightmare* as "an evil spirit formerly thought to oppress people during sleep." Other definitions include "a frightening dream that usually awakens the sleeper."

The Seer's Dictionary defines *nightmare* as "a dream of dark or scary nature inspired by the soul or by demonic powers; a method by which the enemy tempts seers to shut down their dream life."

Nefarious Night Terrors

A night terror is a step up from nightmares. *Merriam-Webster* defines *night terror* as "a sudden awakening in dazed terror that occurs in children during slow-wave sleep, is often preceded by a sudden shrill cry uttered in sleep, and is not remembered when the child awakes." As I share in my book *Decoding Your Dreams*, "Night terrors can bring an all-out panic on the dreamer. Scientists say you may not remember a night terror but when the enemy of your soul is behind the attack you may remember it vividly."

Psalms 91:5 tells us when we fear the Lord, we will not be afraid of the terror at night. And we know God didn't give us a spirit of fear (see 2 Tim. 1:7). But the thief comes to steal, kill, and destroy through terrors.

Witchcraft Dreams

Witchcraft dreams carry witchcraft symbols, like black cats. Cats are associated with evil and witchcraft in most cultures, so it's no wonder a superstition formed about bad luck occurring if a black cat crosses your path. You may dream of other witchcraft symbols or even witches. This could be the Holy Spirit showing you the prophetic witchcraft attack, or it could be because prophetic witchcraft is attacking you while you sleep.

Sleep Paralysis

Sleep paralysis is "a complete temporary paralysis occurring in connection with sleep and especially upon waking," according to *The Merriam-Webster Dictionary*. The medical world acknowledges natural and spiritual implications of sleep paralysis. In fact, WebMD.com writes, "Sleep paralysis is a feeling of being conscious but unable to move. It occurs when a person passes between stages of wakefulness and sleep. During these transitions, you may be unable to move or speak for a few seconds up to a few minutes. Some people may also feel pressure or a sense of choking."

This could happen for natural reasons, but it could also be prophetic witchcraft. This can be beyond scary and defies the Word of God in your life, which promises you can dwell in safety even while you sleep (see Ps. 4:8). Despite all the persecution he endured, the prophet Jeremiah said his sleep was pleasant to him (see Jer. 31:26). So should yours be.

Lacerations on the Body

If you've ever woken up with little scratches all over your body in places your fingernails can't reach, you may be dealing with a unique manifestation of prophetic witchcraft—lacerations on the body. These usually manifest as tiny scratches in batches that are still raw in the morning, or may be scabbed over.

I've had this happen to me more than once. I remember a severe attack like this when I was in Kansas City. A woman who was operating in a Jezebel spirit was on the trip with us. She was dominating all my spare time under the guise of being emotionally disturbed by old traumatic memories. It became frustrating and I finally cut it off. The next morning, I woke up with painful scratches in various parts of my body.

This is usually a sign of someone astral projecting into your room. Unlike God transporting a person in the spirit like He did Philip the evangelist (see Acts 8:26-40), astral projection is the domain of the supernatural realm's dark side, according to *The Seer's Dictionary*. Unlike Philip's experience, astral projection is an at-will, out-of-body experience.

BREAKING PROPHETIC WITCHCRAFT ATTACKS

If you are experiencing prophetic witchcraft attacks, you may be sure you know who or where it's coming from. But remember this: you aren't wrestling against flesh and blood, even though the enemy is using flesh and blood against you. You are wrestling against a power.

You need to put on the whole armor of God and engage in the battle. The armor of God is described in Ephesians 6:14-17:

Stand therefore, having girded your waist with truth, having put on the breastplate of righteousness, and having shod your feet with the preparation of the gospel of peace; above all, taking the shield of faith with which you will be able to quench all the fiery darts of the wicked one. And take the helmet of salvation, and the sword of the Spirit, which is the word of God.

When it comes to witchcraft, we have to withstand it. The Amplified Bible says to "be firm in faith [against his onset—rooted, established, strong, immovable, and determined]" (1 Pet. 5:9 AMPC). It's easy enough to give in to witchcraft, especially if you don't know what is attacking you. So again, when you feel like giving up, when you feel tired for no reason, when you have strong confusion, when you are fighting an intense battle in your mind, and when infirmities are manifesting, it could be witchcraft. Resist it at its onset. Cast it off. Submit yourself to God. "Resist the devil [stand firm against him] and he will flee from you" (James 4:7 AMP).

Again, submit yourself to the lordship of Christ. Exalt His name. Thank Him for His blood. Rejoice in the Lord. Praise and worship carry breakthrough. That's often all it takes to change the spiritual climate in your home. And worship is where we should start because He is worthy of our adoration.

If worship doesn't break the witchcraft, take authority over it in the name above all names. Witchcraft has to bow at the name of Jesus. But make sure you don't have any common ground with the enemy. Repent for any rebellion in your heart, and surrender your will anew to God. Remember, we are more than conquerors in Christ, and no weapon formed against us can prosper—not even witchcraft. Our job is to be spiritually discerning enough to catch the devil at his onset, resist him, rebuke him, and praise God for the victory. Amen.

Remember what Paul said in Second Corinthians 10:3-6:

For though we walk in the flesh, we do not war according to the flesh. For the weapons of our warfare are not carnal but mighty in God for pulling down strongholds, casting down arguments and every high thing that exalts itself against the knowledge of God, bringing every thought into captivity to the obedience of Christ, and being ready to punish all disobedience when your obedience is fulfilled.

CHAPTER 9

SLICK TACTICS OF PROPHETIC
CON ARTISTS

Ephren Taylor II launched a Building Wealth tour that stopped at some of the largest megachurches in America. Taylor pitched his investment plan to the late Bishop Eddie Long's New Missionary Baptist Church in Lithonia, Georgia, and Joel Osteen's Lakewood Church. Long offered him quite the endorsement, saying, "Everything he says is based on the word of God."

Taylor's ponzi scheme was cloaked under the banner of wealth management seminars targeting African-American and Christian communities, according to the U.S. Department of Justice. A ponzi scheme is a form of fraud in which belief in the success of a nonexistent enterprise is fostered by the payment of quick returns to the first investors from money invested by later investors.

Taylor falsely positioned himself as a socially conscious investor and falsely claimed twenty percent of profits were donated to charity. As part of his tour, he met with potential investors, where he sold promissory notes to support small businesses such as laundries, juice bars, and gas stations.

But wait, there's more. Taylor also pushed an investment in sweepstakes machines, with the false claim that the average sweepstakes machine would generate 300 percent investor returns. And he promised the sweepstakes machine investments were 100 percent risk-free. The DOJ determined Taylor knew that the investments he was touting were not profitable and that investors were not receiving actual returns from their investments.

But wait, there's more. Taylor encouraged investors to use self-directed IRAs to make their investments. Many victims transferred their retirement savings to trust companies that acted as custodians for self-directed IRAs, expecting these funds to be used to fund the investments pushed by Taylor. After victims funded their self-directed IRAs, Taylor directed the use of those funds. The money was not invested as promised, but rather was used to pay his business expenses, as well as personal expenses and returns to earlier investors.

In late 2010, the scheme collapsed and Taylor's victims lost virtually all of their investments. The scheme victimized over four hundred people who invested more than $16 million. Taylor was sentenced to nearly 20 years in prison and ordered to pay back the stolen money in restitution after pleading guilty to conspiracy to commit wire fraud.

"This case demonstrates the wide-reaching effects of fraudulent investment schemes and their impact on innocent victims," said Reginald G. Moore, special agent in charge of the United States Secret Service, Atlanta Field Office.[1] "The fact that Ephren Taylor took advantage of people during a time of reverence and trust is particularly heinous."

Taylor may be the most high-profile example of a money scam, but he's far from the only one. Prosperity prophets take Word of Faith teaching to the next level. One such "king prophet" has a following of women who call him "Jesus in the flesh." Leaked video recordings show the prophet—widely known for "money miracles" and selling books of mysteries for $100—engaging in raunchy sex with two women who were not his wife, according to *The Christian Post*.[2]

CBS 12 reported two Florida women allegedly swindled another woman out of her hard-earned money. These "prophets" convinced the woman to hand over her cash so they could pray over it, but then they disappeared with it.[3] Another self-proclaimed prophet in Florida sold followers on the idea of sowing into his ministry in a "pay to pray" scam. He hooked his followers with claims he raised the dead, healed the sick, and promised riches and rewards for those who sowed into his "ministry," according to Fox46.com. A robocall resounded, "I want you to move quickly with a victory seed of $43, or $143, $243 seed. The $1,043 seed."[4]

MIRACLE AND HEALING SCAMS ABOUND

Closely tied to money scams are miracle scams. Call it a trend. I once read about a South African pastor who sprays his congregants—some of them in the face—with insecticide to supposedly heal people. His nickname is "Prophet of Doom." Reuters reported this prophet, named Lethebo Rabalago, said that God can use mud, saliva, or "even poisonous things to deliver people."[5] Reuters also reported on another South African preacher who urged his church to eat grass for healing, as well as drink gasoline to cure what ails them.

I reported on "Prophet" Rufus Phala, who encouraged his church members to drink Dettol, a disinfectant, in order to receive a healing. That's according to *Punch*. In case you aren't familiar, Dettol is a liquid antiseptic and disinfectant that has the potential to cause lethal toxicity. "I know Dettol is harmful, but God instructed me to use it," the false prophet said in a video South Africa's *Daily Sun* ran. "I was the first one to drink it."[6]

> The rise of the so-called "chemical healing" prophets is disturbing but not surprising.
>
> Jesus said to watch out for false prophets—they come to you in sheep's clothing, but inwardly they are ravenous wolves (see Matthew 7:15). Maybe if He had mentioned chemicals, these poor, sickly people would not be falling for error. Then again, when you're desperate to get healed, you'll try just about anything.
>
> Jesus also said false messiahs and false prophets would appear and perform many great signs and wonders (see Matthew 24:24). Phala claimed he has been getting testimonies from people who claiming healing after obeying his orders to imbibe the disinfectant. Somehow, I doubt it.[7]

One YouTube video shows the same woman's broken arm being miraculously healed at church after church. Each time, it was touted as a miracle in several Nigerian churches before the scam was spotted in viral videos. *The Guardian* reports Mrs. Bose Olasukanmi was paid for every successful performance of her trick, which included feigning a broken right arm that no doctor could heal. The arm was twisted and contorted, hanging at her side. The video was so convincing, many of my social media friends shared it on their timelines.

At least five pastors "healed" the woman as the crowd went wild. And the offerings were through the roof as people who were desperate for miracles were encouraged to sow. Some sowed $20,000, $50,000, or more. Others donated their cars.[8]

Meanwhile, a controversial millionaire preacher named Shepherd Bushiri known for miracles and an extravagant lifestyle was arrested in 2020 on alleged fraud and money laundering. He fled from South Africa to Malawi, citing a fear for his life, according to Aljazerra.com.[9]

NOT ALL SCAMS ARE SO OBVIOUS

To many in America, some of these prophetic scams are easy to spot. But false prophets in the West are often more subtle. Indeed, most of the false prophets I see today aren't carrying chemicals. Instead, they are carrying smooth sayings that work to wiggle big money out of small pockets. They are promising weight-loss wonders and money miracles if you sow every last penny in your purse. They are conjuring up fake testimonies for Facebook to prove their anointing.

False prophets and those operating in prophetic witchcraft are also actively working to divide relationships with fabricated accusations rooted in insecurity and pride. When someone demands to be called a general, a grand master bishop, or a most-high-exalted anything, they are straddling the line of a great fall that comes after great pride.

I've said it before, and I'll say it again: I don't think all false prophets start out as false prophets. I think there is a doorway to deception—several doorways, actually. One is greed, another is pride, and there are others we could talk about.

Would that every prophetic person walked circumspectly, minding their Father's business and staying in their area, resisting the temptation to control others and humbly helping the next generation rise up and fill their calling. But the reality is the wheat are growing with the tares, so we're left checking our own hearts and praying for discernment as the false ones keep rising rapidly, giving the prophetic ministry a bad name.

SPOTTING PROPHETIC CON ARTISTS

Jezebel false prophetic con artists want to rob your inheritance—either spiritual or natural. This spirit is a demonic con artist that will shimmy and shake and manipulate you out of what the Lord wants you to have, do, and be. A con artist by definition is someone who cheats, tricks, pressures, or manipulates people into doing something that serves their purposes.

It's not always about money, but it's always about deception. It's about targeting the weak and unsuspecting with the power of persuasion. That manifests as hype, charisma, and a false anointing in Christian circles. It's pure prophetic witchcraft. Flimflam, hustling, grifter prophets and prophetic people earn your trust and then exploit it in a confidence game. These swindling scammers get us because we want to believe what they are offering is true. They play on our emotions, build rapport, and show feigned empathy.

Some of Jezebel's prophetic con artists—people operating in a Jezebel spirit whom the enemy has sent to work you over and out of God's best for your life—launch spiritual attacks. If you have set your heart to advance spiritually, to seek first the Kingdom of God and His righteousness according to Matthew 6:33, look for one of Jezebel's con artists waiting in the wings to thwart your best-laid plans.

I remember when I decided to start getting up at 4 a.m. to seek the Lord. It was radically changing my life for the better. When one of

Jezebel's con artists got wind of my progress, she pulled out all the stops to hinder my bedtime so that I could not rise early in the morning to seek His face. There were unjustified emergencies, false alligator tears, and plenty of guilt heaped on my head if I didn't meet her needs.

Jezebel's con artists also work against your natural inheritance. People operating in this spirit will bleed you dry financially if you let them, taking advantage of your kindness to supply their needs when they should be looking to Christ and His glorious riches. Jezebel's con artists will also work to put a wedge between you and your godly friends who might warn you of her stealth attack against you. So how do you recognize them?

Prophetic con artists are masters of the art of flattery.

We all know Jezebel flatters her victims. Flattery is insincere compliments. It's buttering you up. It's excessive praise. If you are insecure, you will fall for the flattery. I remember when I went to buy a new car because the old one broke down completely. The salesman was complimenting my red hair and found a car he said matched my lovely red hair. Please! Remember, people only flatter you when they want something from you. Don't let Jezebel butter you up and rob from you. Consider these wise words from Proverbs 26:24-28:

> He who hates, disguises it with his lips, and lays up deceit within himself; when he speaks kindly, do not believe him, for there are seven abominations in his heart; though his hatred is covered by deceit, his wickedness will be revealed before the assembly. Whoever digs a pit will fall into it, and he who rolls a stone will have it roll back on him. A lying tongue hates those who are crushed by it, and a flattering mouth works ruin.

Prophetic con artists display false honor.

Essentially another form of flattery, people operating in a Jezebel spirit will honor you with their lips but their heart is far from you (see Matt. 15:8). They pretend to show honor where honor is due, but they are biding their time to strike against you as soon as you don't give them what they want.

I ran into this issue with a young false prophet. He came to me hurt and wounded, and at first appeared beyond honorable. He honored me publicly at every event, bowed before me for prayer, and sowed significant sums of money into my ministry. I knew something was off, but I also knew he was sincerely wounded and hoped I could help him. But the first time I advised him on tasteless self-promotional tactics, he ran and started spewing false accusations and word curses against me.

Listen closely to how people talk about other people. If they are honoring you to your face but speaking ill of other people to you, you can be sure they are slandering you behind your back. Remember what James, the apostle of practical faith, told us:

> *Out of the same mouth proceed blessing and cursing. My brethren, these things ought not to be so. Does a spring send forth fresh water and bitter from the same opening? Can a fig tree, my brethren, bear olives, or a grapevine bear figs? Thus no spring yields both salt water and fresh* (James 3:10-12).

Also remember what Christ said: "A good man out of the good treasure of his heart brings forth good; and an evil man out of the evil treasure of his heart brings forth evil. For out of the abundance of the heart his mouth speaks" (Luke 6:45). The Passion Translation puts it this way: "For the overflow of what has been stored in your heart will be seen by your fruit and will be heard in your words." Fruit takes time to grow. Words are easier to discern.

Prophetic con artists put undue pressure on you.

Prophetic con artists make you feel obligated to cater to their whimsical wishes. Like a bad car salesman, they apply pressure to force your hand—often with time-sensitive requests. High-pressure gimmicks in the church world focus on limited time offers with your seed.

I was in a meeting in Philadelphia where some now well-known false prophets were holding a conference. I didn't know they were false prophets and I was only there to cover the conference for a magazine. When offering time rolled around, there was pressure to "run" to the altar with a seed because only so many people could get the blessing. The urge was "hurry, hurry" as if God's blessings are somehow limited.

I learned a long time ago not to make any decision under pressure, especially a large-scale financial decision. If someone can't wait for me to pray about a purchase or any other matter, the answer is automatically "no." Honest people won't pressure you to do what you aren't sure you should do. If someone is putting pressure on you, let your quick answer be no. And don't waver. As Jesus said, let your no be no (see Matt. 5:37).

Prophetic con artists use illusion and distraction tactics.

They want to distract you from the obvious. It's sort of like the magician who works by sleight of hand. Prophetic con artists have you focusing on what you really want to the point that you can't see what they are really doing. You believe that leg grew out but you didn't notice how the false prophet turned the ankle just enough to bring forth an illusion. David said, "Help me turn my eyes away from illusions so that I pursue only that which is true; drench my soul with life as I walk in your paths" (Ps. 119:37 TPT).

Prophetic con artists use the power of the testimony.

The problem is, they are fabricating testimonies. Money prophets often pay people to come up on stage and share their breakthrough money miracle. Healing prophets do the same thing with false healing testimonies. This aims to build faith in the audience to sow into their own miracle or healing. Exodus 23:1 says plainly, "You shall not circulate a false report. Do not put your hand with the wicked to be an unrighteous witness."

Prophetic con artists are name droppers.

They build credibility with you by dropping names of people they believe will impress you. Mind you, not all name droppers are con artists, but almost every con artist I've ever seen is a name dropper. They hope to get your guard down by their supposed affiliation with a household name. Check references and you'll discover that there is no relationship, or that relationship is strained.

Prophetic con artists use FOMO tactics.

FOMO is the "fear of missing out." Scammers know that one of the key motivators of the human race is fear. That's why you have to accept the offer now—right now.

Prophetic con artists are information seekers.

They want to know intimate details about your life so they can pretend to be your counselor, drawing you to themselves with their empathetic concern about your problems. They are also fishing for information on your financial status or your desperation for breakthrough in some area of your life.

Prophetic con artists won't take no for an answer.

They just keep coming at it from another angle. People who won't accept your "no" are usually trying to control you. If you let them talk you out of your God-inspired "no," you are giving them authority in your life that only belongs to God. People who respect you will respect your "no."

Prophetic con artists feign ignorance or hurt feelings.

If you confront a prophetic con artist, they will act like they have no idea what you are talking about. They'll argue you've misunderstood them, wrongly judged their motives, and the like.

After a speaking engagement in Texas some years ago, someone from the audience Facebook-messaged me offering to sow some marketing help into my ministry. At first, I thought it was an answer to prayer. He said he and his wife really enjoyed the conference and just felt led to help.

I accepted the help and at first all seemed well. There was no money exchanged and he had no access to anything of importance. He was creating social media graphics that were really blessing people who follow my ministry. He started to talk about taking a percentage of new students in my school in exchange for his work and I wasn't opposed to that. However, he said needed access to my back-end financials to calculate it. That was a red flag.

A friend of mine then warned me that he was a convicted con artist using a new name to scam ministries. I Googled it and, lo and behold, it turned out to be true. I immediately confronted him on the findings of financial scams under several corporate names. He insisted that he himself had been scammed by someone else and got dragged into something for which he was now paying restitution.

I wanted to believe him, but what he did next tipped his own hand. He acted like his feelings were hurt. He kept asking, "Who do you think I am?" He started gaslighting me. Gaslighting is a technique that makes you think you are the one with the problem. It's a form of psychological abuse that aims to make you question your own perception of reality. I didn't fall for it. He moved on. And I've since seen him working with other ministries.

Don't be fooled. Prophetic con artists are pretending not to know what they did, but they know exactly what they are doing. Take David's advice, "I do not sit with deceitful men, nor will I go with pretenders" (Ps. 26:4 NASB).

Prophetic con artists offer false concern for your needs.

They may pretend to care about you. They will ask about your family, your health, and so on. They are trying to form a bond with you that will end in you trusting them enough to give them what they want. Indeed, they don't care about you. They only care about what you can do for them or give them.

In Second Timothy 3:13, Paul warned Timothy, "But evil people and impostors will proceed from bad to worse, deceiving and being deceived" (NASB). This description fits people operating in a Jezebel spirit perfectly. They are deceived and being deceived. We cannot tolerate imposters. Paul warned, "You actually allow these imposters to put you into bondage, take complete advantage of you, and rob you blind! How easily you endure those who, in their arrogance, destroy your dignity or even slap you in the face" (2 Cor. 11:20 TPT).

SLICK TACTICS OF PROPHETIC CON ARTISTS

Prophetic con artists promise gifts and favors they don't intend to deliver.

They make big promises, alright, but don't follow through. Solomon spoke of this type: "A person who promises a gift but doesn't give it is like clouds and wind that bring no rain" (Prov. 25:14 NLT).

Prophetic con artists make unsolicited promises and guarantees.

Beware when people say, "I promise." If their word is good, there's no reason to make a promise. You should be hesitant of those who have a habit of making promises. Usually they will either over-promise and under-deliver or won't deliver at all. The promise is a tactic to get your trust. Trust is earned with actions, not with words.

Prophetic con artists conveniently forget what they promised.

Remember, prophetic con artists have no integrity. They make promises they don't intend to keep, then pretend they didn't make them. Know this: Jezebel is a perverse spirit that breathes lies. Proverbs 11:3 reminds, "The integrity of the upright will guide them, but the perverseness of transgressors will destroy them" (MEV).

Prophetic con artists assume and presume on you.

They assume you'll do what they want. They presume you'll bow to their manipulation. What if you didn't?

What if you didn't tolerate Jezebel's prophetic con artists? Ask the Holy Spirit to give you discernment and to help you lean on Him for everything you need. Prophetic con men are experts at spotting and exploiting victims. Be careful about sowing in hyped-up atmospheres with a false anointing called prophetic witchcraft. The seed you sow into a false prophet won't produce the harvest you want.

NOTES

1. U.S. Attorney's Office, Department of Justice, "Ephren Taylor Sentenced to Federal Prison," March 17, 2015, https://www .justice.gov/usao-ndga/pr/ephren-taylor-sentenced-federal-prison.

2. Leonardo Blair, "Texas 'prophet' followers call 'Jesus in the flesh' shown in sex tape with multiple women," The Christian Post, February 25, 2019, https://www.christianpost.com/news/texas -prophet-followers-call-jesus-in-the-flesh-shown-in-sex-tape-with -multiple-women.html.

3. Denise Sawyer, "Fake prophets accused of taking off with cash after 'praying over money' in Okeechobee," CBS12, December 26, 2019, https://cbs12.com/news/local/fake-prophets-accused-of -taking-off-with-cash-after-praying-over-money-in-okeechobee.

4. Matthew Grant, "Pay to pray? A self-proclaimed 'prophet' preying on the faithful," FOX News, February 16, 2019, https://www .fox46.com/news/pay-to-pray-a-self-proclaimed-prophet-preying -on-the-faithful.

5. TJ Strydom and Mfuneko Toyana, "'Prophet of Doom' Banned after Spraying Congregants with Insecticide," *Charisma* News, December 2, 2016, https://www.charismanews.com/ world/61607-prophet-of-doom-banned-after-spraying%7C -congregants-with-insecticide.

6. Jennifer LeClaire, "False Prophet Makes Ill Victims Drink Disinfectant for Miracle Healing," December 16, 2016, https://www.charismanews.com/opinion/watchman-on-the-wall/61887-false-prophet-makes-ill-victims-drink-disinfectant-for-miracle-healing.

7. Ibid.

8. Odita Sunday, "End of road for woman used by 'pastors' to perform fake miracles," *The Guardian,* March 7, 2020, https://guardian.ng/news/end-of-road-for-woman-used-by-pastors-to-perform-fake-miracles.

9. "'Prophet' wanted for fraud flees to Malawi from South Africa," Aljazeera.com, November 14, 2020, https://www.aljazeera.com/news/2020/11/14/prophet-wanted-for-fraud-flees-to-malawi-from-south-africa.

CHAPTER 10

UNMASKING PROPHETIC

MANIPULATORS

I was dealing with a master prophetic manipulator for months and didn't know it. It was all an intentional setup, and the timing was beyond well-orchestrated. The scheme involved a young false prophet, Saul, and an older false prophet, Simon, working together to infiltrate and break up a long-time ministry partnership.

It started when the young false prophet came into my ministry partner Jack's camp. I had a check about Saul and so did other people. But the prophetic manipulator created a soul tie with Jack and started sowing slander seeds against me. He told Jack I had lost respect for him and was working against him. I could feel Jack pulling away and confronted it a few times, but my inquisition didn't yield fruit. I was being stonewalled.

Eventually, Jack discovered Saul was operating in divination and confronted him. When he did, the prophetic manipulator ran to my camp crying about spiritual abuse. Saul pled for my help and covering, telling me all the wicked things Jack supposedly said about me. Some of it was true, but only because of the slander seeds Saul had planted in my friend's mind.

Jack tried to reach out and warn me, but I was so hurt by his previous actions I didn't listen to him. I looked at the presumably wounded Saul and tried to help him. It was Saul who introduced me to an older false prophet, Simon. The older man was savvier, with a slick brand and what appeared to be a tangible anointing.

At first, Simon was a breath of fresh air, but soon I discerned something was off. I couldn't put my finger on it. It was just a feeling. Soon, Simon exposed himself. He started prophesying words over my life I knew weren't accurate. This prophetic witchcraft wasn't merely flattering words but directional words that would benefit him and ultimately derail me. I asked Saul about his elder, and he assured me Simon was above board. But Saul was lying to me. I walked slowly, trying to discern Simon's fruit, but it wasn't long before I saw full-blown manifestations of emotional and financial manipulation in his ministry. The prophetic witchcraft turned my stomach.

God worked it all together for good as I sought His wisdom. Thankfully, I was able to walk away from the situation before my name was sullied and before incurring large losses. Eventually, Jack and I sat down talked and the wicked plot was exposed. The prophetic manipulators succeeded in dividing me and Jack for a time, but not for long. It was a strategic learning experience and one that will serve us both well in the years ahead.

I can tell you—and you may know by experience—how destructive prophetic manipulation is to your soul. Depending on the level of prophetic manipulation, it can also be destructive to your physical body, destructive to your finances, destructive to your career, destructive to your relationships—including your relationship with God. Prophetic manipulation can cause depression and anxiety, dilute your self-confidence, make you feel ashamed or helpless, and even lead you into sinful behaviors to cope with your stress.

God takes manipulation seriously. He said and still means this: "Show your fear of God by not taking advantage of each other. I am the Lord your God" (Lev. 25:17 NLT). And again, "No one should take advantage of and defraud his brother in this matter, because the Lord is the avenger of all such, as we also forewarned you and testified" (1 Thess. 4:6).

UNDERSTANDING MANIPULATION'S MECHANICS

The Merriam-Webster Dictionary defines *manipulation* as "to manage or utilize skillfully; to control or play upon by artful, unfair or insidious means especially to one's own advantage; to change by artful or unfair means as to serve one's purpose." Ultimately, manipulation is a form of witchcraft. Prophetic manipulation falls into the category of prophetic witchcraft. Witchcraft is a work of the flesh listed in Galatians 6.

Rick Joyner has one of the best definitions of witchcraft I've heard: "Witchcraft is counterfeit spiritual authority. It is using a spirit other than the Holy Spirit to dominate, manipulate or control others. Any authority or influence that we gain by our own manipulation or self-promotion will be a stumbling block to us and will hinder our ability to receive true authority from God."

I've fallen victim to manipulation more than once. When you believe the best, it's difficult to believe Christian brothers and sisters would tap into a controlling spirit to attempt to put you under their thumbs, handle you, or otherwise direct your actions. But it happens—and it happens too often. We need to learn, then, not only to discern when people are manipulating us but how to stop the manipulator from succeeding in his nefarious maneuvers—and how to make sure we're not tapping into this work of the flesh ourselves.

Maybe you've run into prophetic manipulators and discerned them up front. Or maybe you've run into prophetic manipulators and discerned them too late—or not at all. It's critical to understand the shenanigans of prophetic manipulators because an enemy exposed is an enemy defeated. You will eventually discern manipulators because resentment will strike your heart. You may feel like you're extending yourself far beyond your natural boundaries to help them—but they aren't there when you need them.

What the manipulator wants at any given time always seems more important than what you need. At some point, your friends may start to point out the manipulation. Listen to your friends. They are seeing something that you aren't. Once you understand their strategies and tactics, you'll never fall for them again. As someone once said, "Characterize people by their actions and you will never be fooled by their words."

You Better Do This or Else!

Prophetic manipulators give you ultimatums. An ultimatum is "a final proposition, condition, or demand," according to *The Merriam-Webster Dictionary*. For example, Simon continued spying on me after I pulled away. I didn't realize he had his minions watching me until, out of the blue, his wife texted me, accusing me of calling out her husband as a false prophet in my church service. She claimed she had the video clip people were sending her.

I knew I had done no such thing and told her she was told wrong or was making major assumptions that I would not entertain. She kept arguing with me and insisting I take down the video (or else). I told her to send me the clip and she did. The clip said nothing about her husband. It was all a guilty imagination and fear that I would expose them because they knew I saw them. She took on a threatening tone with me. I blocked her and moved on. Nothing came of the ultimatum.

I don't bow to ultimatums. It's like negotiating with a terrorist. Once you bow to an ultimatum, you will find yourself in bondage to the prophetic manipulator. Even if they follow through with their threat of leaving, exposing you, or whatever demonic promise they are making, the truth always comes out. God will preserve and protect you. And they will reap what they sow.

Turning On the Charm

Prophetic manipulators may appear charismatic and charming. They are often polite, even delightful. But turning on the charm can be a form of manipulation, even witchcraft. Think of the very meaning of the word *charm*. *Merriam-Webster* defines it as "a trait that fascinates, allures or delights" and "a practice or expression believed to have magic power."

When people turn on the charm, they are compelling, but when the charm is not sincere—when they are literally turning it on and off to manipulate your soul—it's wicked. Proverbs 31:30 warns us, "Charm is deceitful." The one turning on the charm may not be using incantations and spells, but they are nevertheless bewitching you.

You'll notice over time that they can turn off the charm as fast as they turned it on. These manipulators are as two-faced as Dr. Jekyll and Mr. Hyde. They know how to make themselves attractive to their victims, but when the mask comes off you can see their evil intentions. The word "no" often causes the mask to fall off and the intimidation to flow.

Liar, Liar Pants on Fire

Prophetic manipulators are master liars. If you pay attention, you'll notice they tell so many lies they can't keep up with what they told whom. They manipulate with flat-out fabrications of fiction, exaggerations that feed their storyline, misrepresentations of relationships they believe will impress you, white lies, truth distortions, and the like.

Lies are not always one to one or even verbal. Consider how Adolf Hitler's Nazi regime lied to a nation by using propaganda to disguise their political aims. Hitler used lies as allies through compelling poster art that became a weapon of war. Today, prophetic manipulators use social media banners and videos that paint them to be profound miracle workers who cast out demons and never miss it.

Social media propaganda offers the highlight reel of people being slain in the spirit and crumbling in tears after a life-changing prophetic word. Rarely, someone will capture footage of that same prophet rebuking the worship team for being off-key or peeking over a victim's shoulder to read their name or address off the offering check they are holding up to God while the victim's eyes were closed so they can prophesy something particular later in the service.

The Bible has plenty to say about liars, but lying in the name of Jesus is serious business. The psalmist tells us, "He who works deceit shall not dwell within my house; he who tells lies shall not continue in my presence" (Ps. 101:7). And Psalm 52:4 explains how people with deceitful tongues love every word that devours. Prophetic manipulators are inspired by the father of lies, the devil. Don't let the devil manipulate you through a prophet.

Slandering the Discerners

Prophetic manipulators will either shy away from those who may discern their operations—or slander them to discredit them before they share what they see. Prophetic manipulators are on such good behavior in the midst of discerners that they can be difficult to discern. But the real discerner will eventually see them because they watch and pray.

When the prophetic manipulator knows the discerner has caught him, he goes on a smear campaign against them. He projects the flaws of his own soul on to the discerner. That may sound like a "she's a Jezebel" or an accusation that the discerner is actually insecure, jealous, or wounded. The idea is to strip the discerner of his credibility through accusation. This is a tactic of satan's kingdom.

Revelation 12:10 speaks of "the accuser of our brethren, who accused them before our God day and night." We also see satan as accuser in Zechariah 3:1: "Then he showed me Joshua the high priest standing before the Angel of the Lord, and Satan standing at his right hand to oppose him." When a newcomer enters the mix with gossip, slander, and accusation against elders, intercessors, and discerners in your church or circle of friends, let that be a red flag.

Crocodile Tears Flowing Fast

When all else fails, prophetic manipulators let the crocodile tears rip. Crocodile tears are fake tears. It's a false display of crying. Noteworthy is the origin of this phrase, which comes from an ancient belief that crocodiles release tears from their menacing eyes while they are eating their prey.

You've seen crocodile tears if you have children or younger siblings. When a toddler doesn't get what they want, they may wail and scream to get your attention and to compel you to give them what they want. If you give in to the crocodile tears, you're training them to use this manipulation tactic repeatedly.

Prophetic manipulators may not actually cry, but they will display other emotions of grief to prey upon your heart. That could look like depression, loneliness, or desperation. Prophetic manipulators will play on a victim's emotions with sad stories to move their hearts to bend to their will.

Walking on Eggshells

Prophetic manipulators make you feel like you are walking on eggshells. When we walk on eggshells, we're trying especially hard not to make a person angry, upset, or offended.

I was in a church where the apostle was susceptible to fits of anger. You never knew when he was going to explode and surely didn't want to be the target of his wrath. We all learned to walk on eggshells around him, fearful of the backlash for upsetting him. Understand this: questioning prophetic manipulators in any way upsets them.

What we didn't discern at first was this was nothing more than manipulation on this apostle's part. We were afraid of his blow-ups, put-downs, criticisms, and disapproval. According to *Psychology Today*, everyone who is forced to walk on eggshells loses some degree of dignity and autonomy—and half suffer from clinical anxiety or depression. They have trouble sleeping, can't concentrate, can't work as efficiently, and don't enjoy life without drinking. They lack self-esteem.[1]

Playing the Victim Card

Prophetic manipulators play the victim to get your pity. They have sad stories to tell that evoke your empathy, never taking responsibility for anything that went wrong in their life. Their "woe is me" attitude works to elicit your soulish compassion.

In prophetic manipulation circles, this can sound like a plea for money because their television program will be shut down at the end of the week if 1,000 people don't sow $1,000 today. Now, I'm not suggesting everyone who pitches for offerings for their TV show is manipulating you. There are genuine pleas for causes of all sorts. God does bless sowers who plant seed into His Kingdom works. We have to discern the spirit behind the pitch.

Playing the victim card is an attention-getting tactic that serves as bait to catch people who move in a mercy gift but lack discernment. It's like people who stand on the street corner pretending to be homeless. They look the part, but it's a booming business. They live in a house nicer than yours and drive a fancy car. Ultimately, the prophetic manipulators playing the victim card are working to victimize you.

Strings That Make You a Puppet

Prophetic manipulators attach strings to their favor, ultimately turning you into a puppet. Prophetic manipulators may start doing favors out of what seems to be the goodness of their heart, but soon they want to cash in. Beyond friendly reciprocity, they will reveal that the favor was not motivated by kindness but to rope you in. When they tell you "no strings attached"—beware.

British author David Seller once said, "The catch about not looking a gift horse in the mouth is that it may be a Trojan horse." You're familiar with the Trojan horse. The Greeks constructed a monumental wooden horse large enough to house their elite troops. The rolled the Trojan horse up and left it at the gates of the city, then sailed away. The leaders of Troy brought the horse into the city as a victory trophy. The

EXPOSING PROPHETIC WITCHCRAFT

Greek soldiers jumped out and destroyed the city. You might say the Trojan horse came with strings of destruction.

Intimidating Bullies

Prophetic manipulators may work in the realm of intimidation. For most manipulators, intimidation—the use of fear and coercion to get people to do what you want them to do—is not the first tactic. Most prophetic manipulators will first try charm or favors, but if they can't catch the victim with sugar, they'll use vinegar. In other words, if being sweet doesn't work, they will turn into intimidating bullies.

Intimidating bullies may use hints of curses to keep you under their thumb. Veiled and implied threats are part of the mix. Non-verbal intimidations like hostile postures and raised voices are the marks of intimidating bullies. Intimidating bullies may suggest you'll lose your position if you don't comply or, conversely, miss out on an opportunity or promotion.

Spreading a Mob Mentality

Prophetic manipulators may incite others against you in a mob mentality if you don't cooperate with their will. The idea here is to get your peers to pressure you into doing what the manipulator wants. This is called leverage. Those who are already deceived will push you to go along with the crowd. This groupthink or crowd psychology can cause you to think you are the only one who is wrong, and ultimately compel you to bow.

Guilt Trips Galore

Like a child who plays up the fact that you missed their baseball game to get special favors, prophetic con artists will use guilt to get you to perform the way they want. At best, this demonstrates an unforgiving spirit. Remember Romans 8:1, "There is therefore now no condemnation to those who are in Christ Jesus." Don't take on the guilt and condemnation trip.

Skewing the Facts

Prophetic manipulators skew or distort the facts of a situation, reconceptualizing the event to favor their perspective. Their version of the truth is a glorified lie that convincingly defies reality. In their minds, they have so convinced themselves of their version of the story that they cannot be swayed and they will argue the point *ad nauseam*.

Twisting Your Words

Prophetic manipulators twist your words or put words in your mouth that you did not say. The twisted words will shun responsibility for the wrong, shift blame to others for error they promise to correct but never do, turn situations in their favor, or exaggerate the truth to inflate their brand.

Beware the Silent Treatment

An apostle under whom I served once balled me out in front of leadership for something I did not even do. After that, he gave me the silent treatment and the cold shoulder. When he saw me coming, he would intentionally walk the other way or walk by me with glass eyes like he didn't see me. It was a punishment, and it released witchcraft against me.

The silent treatment is a keen strategy among prophetic manipulators. It's carnal at best and demonic at worst. I once offered up this post on my Facebook page:

Did you know the silent treatment (which is the stubborn refusal to talk to someone, especially after a recent argument or disagreement) is a form of witchcraft? Witchcraft is sometimes a spiritual force, but it's also a work of the flesh listed in Galatians. Intimidation is a form of fleshly witchcraft.

Purposely ignoring people to "teach them a lesson" can be a form of fleshly witchcraft. Manipulation tactics, like pouting and crying to get people to do what you want or make them feel guilty, are forms of fleshly witchcraft. I can tell you this, folks won't get far with Spirit-led Christians playing those sorts of flesh-driven games. We'll pray for you but we won't bow to manipulation. 1 Samuel 15:23, "Rebellion to God's Word is as the sin of witchcraft." Trying to punish people with manipulation is rebellion.

Thousands upon thousands of people responded to the post. Most people agreed wholeheartedly with a big "amen." Others had never considered the dynamics of witchcraft as a work of the flesh. Still others didn't quite catch what I meant and asked for clarification. Others quoted verses from Ecclesiastes about how there is a time to speak and a time to stay silent. And at least one person cursed me. Go figure.

Yes, Ecclesiastes 3:7 says there's a time to keep silent and a time to speak. We're to be led by the Holy Spirit, though, not our flesh. It's about motive. Often wisdom dictates staying silent, but the wisdom that is from above is not going to try to use a stubborn silence to pay someone back or teach them a lesson over a petty disagreement. Make sense? Yes, at times Jesus remained silent (see Matt. 26:63), but He was led by the Holy Spirit. He wasn't keeping his lips zipped to punish someone.

Of course, you can wait until you get over the stunned feeling that hit you when you received the message and get your heart in line with God's before you answer. Waiting also gives the person who delivered the questionable message time to cool down or reconsider their stance. Instead of adding fleshly fuel to the fire and letting a poisonous tongue bring division by answering in the same spirit, you can wait until you have peace in your heart and respond out of that peace. You can be a peacemaker who pleases God.

It's all about the motive. If you are letting things cool off, fine. But if you are seeking to punish someone or teach them a lesson with your silence, you're not operating from a godly motive. With that in mind, let's explore what Paul the apostle had to say about works of the flesh.

WICKED WORKS OF THE FLESH

> *Now the works of the flesh are manifest, which are these; Adultery, fornication, uncleanness, lasciviousness, idolatry, witchcraft, hatred, variance, emulations, wrath, strife, seditions, heresies, envyings, murders, drunkenness, revellings, and such like: of the which I tell you before, as I have also told you in time past, that they which do such things shall not inherit the kingdom of God* (Galatians 5:19-21 KJV).

The silent treatment that aims to manipulate or punish people is a work of the flesh because it's disobedient to the Word of God. God doesn't tell us to put a guilt trip on people, manipulate people, try to control people, or the like. We're supposed to walk in love, prefer one another, honor one another, submit ourselves one to another, and for-give one another.

After Saul disobeyed God's word, the prophet Samuel told him, "For rebellion is as the sin of witchcraft, and stubbornness is as iniquity and idolatry" (1 Sam. 15:23). Regarding this verse, *Matthew Henry's Commentary* says:

> It is as bad to set up other gods as to live in disobedience to the true God. Those that are governed by their own corrupt inclinations, in opposition to the command of God, do, in effect, consult the teraphim (as the word here is for idolatry) or the diviners. It was disobedience that made us all sinners (Romans 5:19) and this is the malignity of sin, that it is the transgression of the law, and consequently it is enmity to God, Romans 8:7.

When we try to punish others with the silent treatment, when we work to manipulate people with tears and pouting so they will feel guilty, when we intimidate people, we are essentially practicing a form of witchcraft and idolatry. We're idolizing ourselves and our own wills and our own feelings, and James says, "This wisdom does not descend from above, but is earthly, sensual, demonic" (James 3:15). We're not operating in "the wisdom that is from above is first pure, then peaceable, gentle, willing to yield, full of mercy and good fruits, without partiality and without hypocrisy" (James 3:17). Nor are we operating in the fruit of the Spirit:

> *But the fruit of the Spirit is love, joy, peace, longsuffering, kindness, goodness, faithfulness, gentleness, self-control. Against such there is no law. And those who are Christ's have*

crucified the flesh with its passions and desires. If we live in the Spirit, let us also walk in the Spirit. Let us not become conceited, provoking one another, envying one another (Galatians 5:22-26).

So now, you tell me. Does the silent treatment, intimidation, and manipulation sound more to you like something the Holy Spirit would have you do or fleshly witchcraft? Does it sound like God's wisdom or demonic wisdom? Do we obey God's Word even when we're hurt or mistreated or do we follow the lusts of our flesh unto witchcraft? Selah.

NOTES

1. Steven Stosny, "Walking on Eggshells," *Psychology Today,* December 13, 2019, https://www.psychologytoday.com/us/blog/anger-in-the-age-entitlement/201912/walking-eggshells.

CHAPTER 11

HOW (AND WHEN) TO CONFRONT PROPHETIC

MANIPULATORS

hate confrontation, but it had to be done. For eight years, I was in a spiritually abusive church that operated in a high level of prophetic manipulation. I didn't recognize it at first, because I was a brand-spanking-new born-again believer. I was on fire for God and just wanted to serve Him—and this church welcomed me with open arms.

What I didn't realize was they were not giving me opportunities for the right reasons. Rather, they were building their ministry kingdom on my blood, sweat, and tears. Because I was working as unto the Lord as a baby Christian and didn't discern the motives, I didn't think twice when the work piled on. It started out with me editing articles for the apostle. Later, I would literally rewrite and edit all of his books. I was learning and growing in the process, and it was thrilling.

Soon, I started traveling to other nations producing documentaries. That was when I got my first whiff of prophetic manipulation at the ministry. I felt like I was serving Pharaoh and making bricks without straw. I was on the verge of collapse, working eighteen-hour days in scorching heat trying to please the apostle. I was in physical pain, malnourished, sleep deprived, dehydrated, and the prophetic manipulation sounded like this: "If you faint in the day of adversity, your strength is small."

That's actually a scripture from Proverbs 24:10, but it was twisted to make me feel like I would be seen as a weak, wimpy failure if I didn't complete the project. I wanted to leave the church when I got home, but some elders gave me a speech about suffering for the sake of Christ. I was such a new believer, I bought into it and kept serving. Soon, I was doing so much media work on top of my full-time entrepreneurial exploits that I was approaching burnout.

As a single mother with many responsibilities and more bills to pay, I couldn't keep up with the demand for Monday morning meetings at the church. It was an unreasonable expectation, and eventually I dropped the ball because I got sick. The apostle called me, cursed me, and demanded I get to the church immediately or else. His ultimatum did not bear fruit. I was literally unable to go and his words just made me sicker.

In this church, you had to ask permission to visit your family at Christmas. People had to ask permission to get married. There were many secrets, many cold shoulders, many controlling tactics and unspoken rules we'd be punished for breaking. I watched person after person leave the church only to be verbally crucified in front of the congregation. I was afraid to leave and afraid to stay. Eight years later, I had enough. I didn't know exactly what I was dealing with, but I knew it wasn't God.

The Lord told me, "Go in peace." But two of my friends in the church insisted that I speak with the apostle and his wife. The thought of it terrified me, but I decided I would tell them everything I was feeling. I decided I would share how outside counselors told me how I was being treated was abusive and advised me to leave. I was hoping they would repent, but if not at least I did the right thing. As it turns out, the church leaders refused to meet with me. They told the congregation I lost my salvation and became a false prophet, a victim of Jezebel.

Looking back, I'm grateful I never had that confrontation. It would not have gone well with me. They would have spewed even more curses and tried to tear me apart on the way out the door. Ten years later, people still come to my church, Awakening House of Prayer in Ft. Lauderdale, and tell me the leadership curses me publicly. I have had to learn to walk in forgiveness, and I also learned that sometimes it's not the best idea to confront a prophetic manipulator. Like a bad movie, sometimes you just have to fade out and not look back.

Other times, though, you have to confront the prophetic manipulation. Sometimes, you just have no choice. The Holy Spirit leads you to do it, sometimes for their sake more than yours. He wants them to break free and will use you as an Elijah in a showdown that hopes to see them repent. If that happens, don't be afraid. Rather, remember the words in Luke 12:11-12: "Now when they bring you to the synagogues and magistrates and authorities, do not worry about how or what you should answer, or what you should say. For the Holy Spirit will teach you in that very hour what you ought to say."

BEFORE YOU CONFRONT PROPHETIC MANIPULATORS

So how do you respond when you are led to respond? What do you do when you've realized that you've been under the thumb of an emotional manipulator? How do you break free? The first step is to recognize the prophetic manipulation. You won't want to see it. It's painful to see it. It will make you angry to see it.

Ask God to break deception off your mind so you can see through the plots and plans of prophetic manipulators. As I always say, an enemy exposed is an enemy defeated. When you see it, a righteous indignation will arise in you and you will stop tolerating it. You may need to get some outside perspective on the issue. Your goal is not to slander or expose a person but to see the prophetic manipulation for what it is. Many times when you are under the cloud of prophetic witchcraft, you can't see straight.

The next step is to repent. Ask God to forgive you for coming under a false authority. Yes, we are called to walk in love (see Eph. 5:2) and prefer one another (see Rom. 12:10), but that doesn't mean we have to allow someone to make us emotional slaves. There's a difference. For freedom Christ set us free (see Gal. 5:1).

You can't bow to a witchcraft spirit and bow to the Holy Spirit at the same time. Repent for the time and money you've sowed when you fell into manipulation. Repent for not discerning what the Holy Spirt was trying to show you, because I can tell you for sure He was trying to show you. Ask the Lord to show you how you fell into the prophetic manipulator's schemes. Is there insecurity in your heart, ambition? Are you too naïve? Do you need to sharpen your discernment skills? Paul wrote these words to a church in Corinth:

> *Now I rejoice, not that you were made sorry, but that your sorrow led to repentance. For you were made sorry in a godly manner, that you might suffer loss from us in nothing. For godly sorrow produces repentance leading to salvation, not to be regretted; but the sorrow of the world produces death. For observe this very thing, that you sorrowed in a godly*

manner: What diligence it produced in you, what clearing of yourselves, what indignation, what fear, what vehement desire, what zeal, what vindication! In all things you proved yourselves to be clear in this matter (2 Corinthians 7:9-11).

Next, forgive yourself. Once you see the depth of the manipulation, you'll probably be angry with yourself or feel dumb for falling into the emotional manipulator's trap. Forgive yourself (see 1 John 1:9). It can happen to anyone. You've got a kind, loving heart, and you believed the best. You may have a mercy gift that you need to balance with righteous judgment. Just learn a lesson and stop the abuse.

Finally, prepare for potential backlash. Your words may not be well-received and you may get an earful from their mouthful. Go into the confrontation prayed up and emotionally ready to deflect the negative reactions and words spoken to and about you. At times, you may need to have someone as a witness for your own emotional protection.

DEFLECTING PROPHETIC MANIPULATORS

You may not have to actually confront the prophetic manipulator if you learn how to deflect the manipulation. If you consistently deflect, the prophetic manipulator will give up and go somewhere else, like the con man who is found out. This is your best case scenario, so it's worth employing some of these handy dandy techniques.

Some techniques are more appropriate than others, depending on the situation in which you find yourself. Sometimes two or more of these techniques can be used in combination. Remember, "The heart of the righteous studies how to answer, but the mouth of the wicked pours forth evil" (Prov. 15:28).

Keep your distance.

Start pulling away from the prophetic manipulators. It's not always necessary to make an announcement of your departure. Just don't answer every text and phone call. Don't go to their meetings. Decline their invitations. They will probably get the hint. They will know you see them, but may not see you as a threat if you just stop coming around. In many cases, this is your best outcome.

Learn to offer a diplomatic "no."

Saying "no" is a hard word for many people, but it's a word you need to learn to appreciate and deploy. No is a word of refusal, it is a denial of someone's request, it is declining to cooperate. Say it with me: "No." You don't have to be mean-spirited about your no, but you do need to be confident and settled on the no or the prophetic manipulator will talk you into a yes.

Know this in advance: emotional manipulators may get angry when you stop catering to their every need and stand up for yourself, but stick to your guns. Just politely but firmly tell them no, more than once if you have to.

You are not obligated to give anybody a reason for your no, and it's better not to because they will argue and work to sway your opinion with more prophetic manipulation. Like the Bible says, let your yes be yes and your no be no (see Matt. 5:37). Don't apologize for your no. You're really not sorry, or at least you shouldn't be.

Ask what they really want.

I got a phone message from someone who caused me a lot of trouble in my life. He was brash with poor character and controlling, even though he moved in signs and wonders. A former crackhead, I gave him lots of grace but eventually had to distance myself for my own wellbeing. Years after I politely backed out, the voice message suggested that God told him I was supposed to call him. Guess what? That call was never returned. God didn't tell me that. God didn't tell him that either. It was prophetic manipulation. He hadn't changed a bit after all those years.

Here's the point: he wanted something from me. Prophetic manipulators always want something from you. Always. They may beat around the bush. They may come at it in subtle ways. They may offer you this, that, and the other favor as a setup for their big ask. Cut to the chase with prophetic manipulators so you don't sucked in. Ask them what they really want and then ask the Lord what He wants you to do.

Ask pushback questions.

What are pushback questions? Questions that push the onus back on the prophetic manipulator to rethink their tactics. These are questions like, "Does this seem reasonable to you?"; "Are you really expecting me to do this for you?"; and, "Do I get to have an opinion here?" Many times, manipulators will back down. Other times, they will argue their case. Like Paul told Timothy, don't argue back (see 2 Tim. 2:23).

Deploy a time buffer.

When the manipulator asks you to do something for them that's unreasonable, use these four words: "I'll think about it." This is less dramatic than saying no and can help you avoid the manipulator's wrath. A soft answer, as Solomon said, turns away wrath (see Prov. 15:1).

Set up clear boundaries.

Boundaries. You can't see them, but you can certainly draw them—and you need to. I understand because I've been there—and I try not to keep going back. I've had to learn the hard way (and by "hard way" I mean from the pain of burnout) how to limit who gets close to me. I am careful about with whom I share what information. I set boundaries around times of the day people can expect a response from me. Indeed, I have had to practice the art of boundary setting. You should too.

TECHNIQUES TO CONFRONT PROPHETIC MANIPULATORS

Just like a bully on the playground, emotional manipulators sometimes need to be confronted. This may sound scary to you, but remember God did not give you a spirit of fear but of power, love, and a sound mind (see 2 Tim. 1:7).

If you hope to save the relationship, the manipulator needs to be made aware of his tactics and given a space to repent. Remember, Jesus even gave Jezebel a space to repent (see Rev. 2:21). However, if the only relationship you have with the prophetic manipulator is one of service—in other words, if it's not a deep, personal, committed relationship—the best move is to call it like you see it knowing you'll likely have to move on because, like Jezebel, the prophetic manipulator usually will not repent and the confrontation may bring more backlash that you are ready to handle.

There are many ways to confront prophetic manipulators. Some of them are more aggressive than others. Remember, always ask the Holy Spirit to show you if, when, and how to respond to prophetic manipulators. Again, sometimes you just need to walk away, block their social media accounts, and take other measures to lock them out of your life.

Know your rights.

You have the right as a child of God to be treated respectfully and to express your opinions and points of view respectfully. You have the right to say no, to disagree without being shamed, guilted, or condemned. You have the right to protect yourself from emotional, physical, or mental manipulation. You have the right to follow the Holy Spirit and ultimately have a responsibility to submit to His leadership. Be confident in who you are and your rights before you go into the confrontation.

Expect but don't enter the argument.

Come in with facts in hand that the prophetic manipulator can't deny. If they do deny the facts, don't argue. It's just a means of prophetic manipulation to wear you down. Stick to your guns and don't give in to the temptation to defend yourself as they turn the tables on you, because they inevitably will. Don't be surprised if they accuse you of manipulation, control, having a spirit of rejection, or some other instability. Don't be surprised if they deploy more prophetic manipulation to bribe you with some position or opportunity. If the situation escalates, exit the conversation.

Point to God's Word.

No one can argue with God's Word. They may try to pretend like they are walking in love and honoring people. They may reject everything you say. But if you stand on God's Word and speak the truth in love, without resentment, you are at least sowing seeds in their soul that set the stage for Holy Spirit conviction. Remember, you are not the convincer. That is the Holy Spirit's job.

Know when to cut ties.

If the manipulator will not repent, it may be time to cut ties. Often, emotional manipulators create soul ties with their victims by finding their weaknesses and ministering to their needs before they start making demands. It can be difficult to cut loose. Other times, as in marriages, you can't always cut loose. Pray and ask the Holy Spirit to bless the manipulator with a revelation of His love and truth, and ask Him if you should stick it out or break ties with your manipulating friend.

This is certain: if they don't repent, the situation will escalate. They will work to slander and discredit you in whatever relationships or organizational interests you share. They will try to make your life miserable behind the scenes. If you haven't already cut ties by that time, sever them immediately. God is your vindicator (see Ps. 43:1).

CONFRONTATION IN ACTION

Let me show you a real life example of how I handled a prophetic manipulator who was wooing the young adults in my church—as well as some of the elders. As I mentioned, he had a handful of my staff doing volunteer work for his ministry. The prophetic manipulator convinced them I knew about it. He bewitched them. I started pulling back while I chose how to handle it.

During the launch of the first book in this series, *Discerning Prophetic Witchcraft*, I was doing a series of prayer calls and teaching videos about prophetic witchcraft. I am not sure if it was his conscience or the

Holy Spirit convicting him, but he went on the war path. He sent me a text full of lies and prophetic manipulation. He was accusing me of publicly calling him out as a false prophet and going behind his back in secret to make such accusations. I assured him I had not done this and that these calls and videos were in conjunction with my book launch. But he persisted. His final text read:

> I heard rumors from people (didn't believe it) so I approached you directly as Scripture says... Some of the people we met through you at your last event reached out to ask us questions of which we didn't respond because it would be wrong to do so; some unfriended us and unfollowed our ministry. I went back and listen to your prayer call and you painted a pretty clear picture there too. I've not accused you of anything; questions aren't accusations.
>
> You've refused to answer direct questions. No one is above questions; me asking you direct questions isn't disrespectful; it's the right thing to do. You invested in our lives and we genuinely love and served you...and God knows and sees all things; expected nothing in return but prayers over us.
>
> I don't have any past hurt, even this doesn't hurt me...if I did something wrong; I would like to learn, grow and move forward but if more than two people approach you that I directly or indirectly said anything bad about you; I would hope you would call me directly.
>
> I prophesy and pray for people as though my life depends on it because one day I will stand before God and give account for every single word I spoke and every action...if I heard that a million people painted us as false prophets;

I won't care but they mentioned you; there's too much love between us for me not to ask. I won't disrespect you ever; it will invalidate all the good you did for us and vice versa but I will follow the scriptural path to resolving this issue asking you again:

1. Are we false prophets? If so what did we do wrong and what do we need to do to fix it. 2. Did you directly or indirectly advice people not to follow our ministry? 3. Did I/we offend you in any way or step out of line? 4. Did you unfriend me or was that your algorithm? If you choose not to answer my questions; It's ok. I wouldn't want to sin against God over this matter so I'm going to leave it alone.

Now, notice how he's using Scripture to justify his continual confrontation. He was lying about the people at my event, as I had not told anyone about his activities. I was trying to fade out without massive warfare, but he wouldn't take no for an answer. He continued to insist my prayer calls were about him, which they weren't. He accused me of "refusing to answer direct questions" as if I have to submit to his witchcraft.

Next, he pulled back and expressed his appreciation. He wasn't pressuring me for information so he could learn and grow. He was probing to try to get ahead of the collateral damage by pushing me to affirm his suspicions. He started calling all the people in my church that same day, trying to get ahead of the game. But they had since repented and seen how he manipulated them and lied to me and would not respond.

Finally, he continued to act as if he cared what I thought and respected me, which is obviously not true because he lied to my face on several occasions and was caught in his own trap. He continued to press me to answer questions that I had previously chosen not to dignify because the questions were nothing more than accusations. He continued acting as if he was trying to obey God, when there were mountains of evidence of his prophetic manipulation.

Here's my response:

> Please give me their names and I will follow up with them directly. One would think you'd want to defend me if I am your mother and apostle. Your strong language is very troublesome. I haven't refused to do anything. You have, though, declined repeatedly to give the names of the people you keep pointing back to that spurred you to start this line of questioning. I understand also that you want all this in writing.
>
> At this point, I think it's best if we choose to walk separate paths peacefully. Maybe we can try to talk after the dust settles. I would urge you to pray and seek the Lord. Right now, this is going nowhere and each one of your messages is worse than the last. It's not wisdom to continue down these lines and the Holy Spirit has advised me not to engage further. Please do not message me again regarding this issue.

And that was the end of it. Later I found out he had left a landlord in another nation high and dry and was using some prophetic manipulators in another foreign nation as part of his scam to defraud God's people. It was an elaborate international network, which is sure to fail because he's good at manipulation but poor at covering his tracks. Most wolves are.

CHAPTER 12

DIVINERS, FALSE PROPHETS, AND PROPHETIC
WITCHES

I've been troubled in my spirit for some time over what I call the "monthly prophecy" trend. We see prophets—and even those who don't claim to be prophets—releasing a brand-spanking-new, shiny, happy prophetic word chock-full of super-duper life-changing promises each and every month.

You'll hear them prophesy "it's the month of this" or "the month of that" or "the month of the other." Every first of the month, without fail, they have a freshly minted prophetic word for the Body of Christ. Not just one, but scores and scores and scores of monthly prophetic words circulate social media. Many people are anticipating them with great excitement!

The problem is most of those prophecies fail. They fall right to the ground with a loud thud that echoes. The prophetic word did not prosper because it did not come out of God's mouth. Rather, it returned void. And yet the very next month, these social media prophets—motivated by clicks, likes, and CashApp cha-chings—pontificate about prophetic promises that must surely come to pass in a thirty-day window. Is there no shame?

I was writing entries for my *Seer's Dictionary* when I came across this Scripture that made my jaw drop. We find it in Isaiah 47:13-14:

> *You are wearied in the multitude of your counsels; let now the astrologers, the stargazers, and the monthly prognostica-tors stand up and save you from what shall come upon you. Behold, they shall be as stubble, the fire shall burn them; they shall not deliver themselves from the power of the flame; it shall not be a coal to be warmed by, nor a fire to sit before!*

What is a prognosticator, you ask? One who foretells from signs and symptoms, according to *The Merriam-Webster Dictionary*. Here's how it works: one of the monthly prophets felt the wind blow, and suddenly it's the month of the wind of God. God didn't say it, but it tickles people's ears and loosens their purse strings.

The New Living Translation reads, "All the advice you receive has made you tired. Where are all your astrologers, those stargazers who make predictions each month? Let them stand up and save you from what the future holds." And the Contemporary English Version, "You have worn yourself out, asking for advice from those who study the stars and tell the future month after month."

ARE THE "PROPHETS" PRACTICING WITCHCRAFT?

This "monthly prophetic word" trend has troubled me for a long while. I understand a sermon series based on a prophetic word. I did that for a few months several years ago as part of preaching series for my church, Awakening House of Prayer. When the Lord stopped, I stopped. I also understand sending out prophetic encouragement each month to those who follow your ministry. That's healthy, but it can come very close to prophetic witchcraft if one feels pressured to produce a new monthly word every thirty days.

What troubles me are the grandiose promises from scores of people each and every month that come with an unspoken guarantee that it will happen in that thirty-day window. Without fail, every single September someone prophesies it's a "September to Remember." Some prophesy every October how it's month of harvest with strong instructions to sow. The only one who got a harvest was the prophet who prophesied it.

I have often wondered things like, *Which one of these prophets are we supposed to believe?* I sense people's heads are spinning at the beginning of the month, or should I say twirling, trying to determine which prophet to believe so they can prosper. I have often pondered if anyone judges these prophecies, or is the hype they feel in the moment worth the disappointment that comes on the 30th of the month when the word returned void?

Is this monthly prophecy trend bordering on divination? Is it witchcraft? Again, I believe it's a fine line and a true prophet can slip into a false practice, especially when under pressure. I do believe God is speaking continually and always has something new to say, but when we try to confine God's word to a Gregorian calendar month after month, we're in danger of tapping into divination.

A WARNING ABOUT DIVINERS

Before I was born again, I was in desperate search of truth. I did not know what to do, so I went to palm readers, crystal readers, and even called the psychic hotline Miss Cleo and ran up my phone bill. I don't think I actually spoke to Miss Cleo. She had quite a racket going on with lots of psychics on staff answering ringing phones.

Miss Cleo was super popular in the 1990s, appearing on late night TV with a deck of tarot cards, candles, and the urge to "Call me now!" Apparently, her Jamaican accent was fake and was exposed in lawsuits. According to *The New York Times*, a federal lawsuit ordered Psychic Readers Network and Access Resource Services, who ran Cleo's commercials, to forgive $500 million customer fees. Miss Cleo, whose real name was Youree Dell Harris, died of cancer at age 53.[1]

When I got saved, I renounced all alignment and every word from psychics. Most blood-bought, born-again, Bible-reading, tongue-talking, demon-busting Christians are not going to go to someone like Miss Cleo, but they don't discern prophetic witchcraft when it comes from inside the church—or at a Christian conference or on a Facebook Live with the title, "Can I prophesy?" (Read *Discerning Prophetic Witchcraft* to learn more about how to discern what I am exposing in this sequel.)

Ploys like Miss Cleo's psychic hotline are blatant to most Christians. But false prophets come as wolves dressed in sheep's clothing. There's not much difference, though, between Miss Cleo and the false prophets. They may dress different. They may use different terminology. But they are all operating in prophetic witchcraft. That's why John warned us to test the spirits (see 1 John 4:1).

Diviners speak when God is not speaking. Ezekiel 22:28 reveals, "And her prophets have smeared whitewash for them, seeing false visions and divining lies for them, saying, 'Thus says the Lord God,' when the Lord has not spoken" (ESV). Diviners will lead you where you want to go—or where they want you to go—instead of where God wants you to go. And they will usually charge you a pretty penny for the journey.

Just as psychics keep you on the line, coming back to pay more money for more insight, crystals, and cards, false prophets keep you on the line with false prophecy until they can bait you and reel you all the way into their net. If someone comes against these diviners, they threaten to file a lawsuit. I received an e-mail once from a well-known false prophet who operates in twisted theologies and is all about the money. The email offered threats over an article we posted on awakenigmag.com. The letter read:

> It has come to our attention that you have participated with [name of magazine, name of author, name of publisher], in their unprofessional and slanderous journalism against [name of false prophet]. The source of their article is a man...who is currently under investigation by the FBI for his crimes and death threats that he has released and influenced against [false prophet] and his ministry.
>
> [The publisher] and [the article's author] were informed of this before they published their ridiculous article, but they did not listen. You too are being informed about the situation. If you do not remove the article from your website...your name and ministry will also be submitted to the FBI for investigation.
>
> Not only that, but these two videos below will be made public to the Body of Christ, just like you made public an evil and false report for no good reason. You have

never met [name of false prophet]. Who are you to speak against the Lord's servant when you haven't even taken the time to ever reach out to him? You don't know him or his ministry, and yet you take up a sword against him without cause. You need to repent.

There was a short version and a long version of the video, which were full of lies, spliced footage, cover ups, false testimonies from the false prophet's PR team, and other slanderous accusations. Do you think I was afraid? No way. I am not afraid of false prophets and neither should you be. I stand on these words in Deuteronomy 18:20-22:

> *"But the prophet who presumes to speak a word in My name, which I have not commanded him to speak, or who speaks in the name of other gods, that prophet shall die." And if you say in your heart, "How shall we know the word which the Lord has not spoken?"—when a prophet speaks in the name of the Lord, if the thing does not happen or come to pass, that is the thing which the Lord has not spoken; the prophet has spoken it presumptuously; you shall not be afraid of him.*

I didn't respond, nor did I remove the article from my site. And I never heard anything from the false prophet again. Beyond the warnings to diviners, though, God also warns those who support them—and even chase after them.

A WARNING TO THOSE CHASING PROPHECY

When I minister in certain nations, I am literally bombarded with people wanting a prophetic word—and it's not always in other nations. I was at a conference in Arizona and got up at 5 a.m. to hit the gym before my plane took off. A woman who was at the conference must have seen me go into the fitness center and waited an entire hour until I came out. She was standing outside the door when I exited.

"What a blessing that I ran into you," she said. "It was the Lord who ordered my steps because you have a prophetic word for me." I was taken aback. I didn't immediately know how to respond to such an imposition wrapped in a lie. The Lord didn't order her steps to the frame of the gym door to stalk me for a word, and I honestly didn't have a word for her. She had already received many prophetic words that weekend and just wanted one more.

Since then, I've been in similar situations over and over again. It's rare that I go anywhere that people don't come up to me and announce that the Lord told them I have a word for them, then proceed to pull out their phone and hit the record button, close their eyes and posture their arms in a receiving mode. I am not upset with the people. I am upset with their pastors who don't equip them to hear the voice of God.

Here's why: believers who chase prophets and prophecy are more prone to fall into a prophetic witchcraft trap. The Lord loves them, but chasing after prophets for prophecy doesn't please Him. He wants a personal relationship with each one of us. Part of the reason Jesus died on the cross was to tear the veil between heaven and earth and give us the right to boldly approach the throne of grace and petition the Father in His name.

Chasing prophets and personal prophecy cuts God out of the immediate equation. Even if the prophetic word is true, God doesn't want you to be dependent on anyone but Him for direction. Of course, God sends prophets to prophesy to us, but that's His choice not ours. Our aim should be to discover how to discern the voice of God for ourselves. After all, there won't always be a prophet around.

God doesn't want us to fall into a pit of witchcraft. He warned His people, "Give no regard to mediums and familiar spirits; do not seek after them, to be defiled by them: I am the Lord your God" (Lev. 19:31). Put in today's language, that might read, "Don't chase prophets and prophecy because you might not get a pure word from My heart. I am the Lord your God and I want to speak to you Myself."

Remember King Saul? He did a lot of things wrong, but he did do some things right. After Samuel died, Saul evicted all the diviners from Israel and when the Philistines gathered together to fight his army Saul turned to the Lord for help: "And when Saul inquired of the Lord, the Lord did not answer him, either by dreams or by Urim or by the prophets" (1 Sam. 28:6).

Saul was on the right track, but he wasn't willing to wait on the Lord. He was hungry for a word and he backslid. Saul told his servants to find a diviner so he could go make an inquiry. Saul put on a disguise and went to the diviner by night asking her to conduct a séance and bring up Samuel from the dead. First Chronicles 10:13-14 tells of the evil king's fate:

> So Saul died for his breach of faith. He broke faith with the Lord in that he did not keep the command of the Lord, and also consulted a medium, seeking guidance. He did not seek guidance from the Lord. Therefore the Lord put him to death and turned the kingdom over to David the son of Jesse (ESV).

You are probably not going to be tempted to go to the local palm reader or ask a psychic to conduct a séance, but when you pay for prophecy it's not much different in the eyes of the Lord. When you eat at the table of a false prophet you are digesting divination and it will not lead to life. The power in divination words may sound like life, but they ultimately lead you astray. The devil may prophesy to you through someone who carries the title of the prophet, and it may sound good, but the end is not God's will.

A WARNING TO DIVINERS

God warns us in His Word about divination and the like because He's a merciful God. Until their dying breath, anyone can repent of prophetic witchcraft or even intentional false prophetic operations because of the blood of Jesus and the New Testament covenant. In the Old Testament the punishment was swifter. False prophets were stoned and witches were not permitted to live (see Exod. 22:18). Thank God for His blood.

Still, the colorful warnings God inspired the true prophets to record in the books that are now part of our Bible should help us understand God's emotions about prophetic witchcraft. Leviticus 19:26 warns the Israelites not to practice divination or soothsaying. And Leviticus 20:27 makes the Old Testament paradigm clear, "A man or a woman who is a medium, or who has familiar spirits, shall surely be put to death; they shall stone them with stones. Their blood shall be upon them."

At this point, you might ask, "Why does prophetic witchcraft make Him so angry?" It makes God angry because it leads people away from His heart. It deceives people and ruins lives. It destroys marriages and tempts people to chase idols. It grieves His Spirit because the devil is behind prophetic witchcraft and He loves you too much to see you fall into the hands of the thief.

Apparently, the Israelites didn't take the warning seriously. Nearly one thousand years after Moses scribed prophetic warning after prophetic warning, prophetic witchcraft was still running rampant in Israel. Ezekiel offers a strong prophecy against witches. Let the colorful language in Ezekiel 13:18-19 sink in:

> *Thus says the Lord God: "Woe to the women who sew magic charms on their sleeves and make veils for the heads of people of every height to hunt souls! Will you hunt the souls of My people, and keep yourselves alive? And will you profane Me among My people for handfuls of barley and for pieces of bread, killing people who should not die, and keeping people alive who should not live, by your lying to My people who listen to lies?"*

What's going on here? These witches are soul hunting. Jezebel's prophets and other false prophetic operators are soul hunting today. They use prophetic witchcraft with smooth sayings and flattering words to hook souls like a piece of bologna hooks a catfish. In exchange, they are paid with barley and bread. The result—people who live should die and people who die should live. It's all lies, and God releases woe, which is judgment, upon them.

Ezekiel 13:20-23 continues:

> *Therefore thus says the Lord God: "Behold, I am against your magic charms by which you hunt souls there like birds. I will tear them from your arms, and let the souls go, the souls you hunt like birds. I will also tear off your veils and deliver My*

people out of your hand, and they shall no longer be as prey in your hand. Then you shall know that I am the Lord.

Because with lies you have made the heart of the righteous sad, whom I have not made sad; and you have strengthened the hands of the wicked, so that he does not turn from his wicked way to save his life. Therefore you shall no longer envision futility nor practice divination; for I will deliver My people out of your hand, and you shall know that I am the Lord."

Look here at how much the Lord loves His people. He rescued them from the prophetic witchcraft and exposed the diviners. Despite the warning—despite His people chasing false prophets and prophecy—God showed mercy on His people and shut down the works of darkness. But also notice that He did not show mercy on the diviners. They were also warned and rejected the wisdom of the Lord. They continued in the unfruitful works of darkness and experienced a payday on the wages of sin.

DIVINERS ARE GOING TO HELL

God is the same yesterday, today, and forever. Although the covenant changed when Jesus died on a cross to pay the price for our sins, God's views on diviners, false prophets, and prophetic witches stayed constant. He hates divination and issues strong words to diviners throughout the Scripture.

This is what the Lord says: "You false prophets are leading my people astray! You promise peace for those who give you food, but you declare war on those who refuse to feed you. Now the

*night will close around you, cutting off all your visions. Dark-
ness will cover you, putting an end to your predictions. The
sun will set for you prophets, and your day will come to an
end. Then you seers will be put to shame, and you fortune-tell-
ers will be disgraced. And you will cover your faces because
there is no answer from God"* (Micah 3:5-7 NLT).

The Old Testament has an abundance to say about false prophets,
diviners, witches, sorcerers, mediums, necromancers, and those who
deal in familiar spirits. But lest we conclude God feels differently about
these practices in the New Testament, let's look at the end of the book.

*He who overcomes shall inherit all things, and I will be his
God and he shall be My son. But the cowardly, unbelieving,
abominable, murderers, sexually immoral, sorcerers, idolaters, and all liars shall have their part in the lake which burns
with fire and brimstone, which is the second death* (Revelation 21:7-8).

And here's your second witness. Revelation 22:14-15 reads:

*Blessed are those who do His commandments, that they may
have the right to the tree of life, and may enter through the
gates into the city. But outside are dogs and sorcerers and
sexually immoral and murderers and idolaters, and whoever
loves and practices a lie.*

God is saying that false prophets, diviners, witches, sorcerers, mediums, necromancers, and those who deal in familiar spirits will go to hell
if they don't repent. With that in mind, it's important from the get-go

to define what a false prophet is. As I explained in the first book in this series, *Discerning Prophetic Witchcraft*:

> A false prophet is not one who misses it or one who makes poor judgment calls in ministry operations as they learn and grow. No, a false prophet, in the simplest terms, is one who sets out to deceive. The motive is to gain something to consume upon their own lusts outside the will of God, whether that's money, fame, or some other reward. They don't seek God for what they need, but rather they manipulate their way into what they want.

As I've mentioned—and it bears repeating—Paul warned about the fate of false ministers in Second Corinthians 11:13-15, "For such men are false apostles, deceitful workmen, disguising themselves as apostles of Christ. And no wonder, for even Satan disguises himself as an angel of light. So it is no surprise if his servants, also, disguise themselves as servants of righteousness. Their end will correspond to their deeds" (ESV). Peter continued, "And in their greed they will exploit you with false words. Their condemnation from long ago is not idle, and their destruction is not asleep" (2 Pet. 2:3 ESV).

And Jesus gave us a second warning about false prophets in the end times in Matthew 24:11: "Then many false prophets will rise up and deceive many." Notice the double use of the word *many*. It doesn't say "a few false prophets will rise up and deceive unbelievers." It doesn't say "many false prophets will rise up and deceive a few." It paints a picture of a vast number of false prophets deceiving a vast number of people. In fact, the Greek word for *many* in that verse is *polus*. *HELPS Word Studies* defines it as "many (high in number); multitudinous, plenteous, much, great in amount (extent)."

Consider yourself warned, and ask the Holy Spirit.

NOTE

1. "Youree Dell Harris, the TV Psychic Miss Cleo, Dies at 53," *New York Times,* https://www.nytimes.com/2016/07/27/business/media/tv-psychic-miss-cleo-dies.html.

CHAPTER 13

PROTECTING YOURSELF (AND YOUR SHEEP) FROM

THE WOLVES

Wolves are not just within the four walls of the church—wolves are everywhere. Whether you are leader of a church, a leader of a business, a leader of your home, or a leader in any capacity, you are serving as a shepherd. And one of the shepherd's jobs is to protect the sheep from the wolves. I'm reminded of one of Aesop's Fables, *The Wolf in Sheep's Clothing*. Although short, it speaks volumes to leaders hoping to protect their people from prophetic witchcraft. It reads:

> One day a wolf found a sheep's skin. He wrapped himself in it and sneaked into a sheep pen. He ate a lamb. He was sneaking up on a second lamb when the shepherd caught him.
>
> "Don't throw me out," said the wolf. "I'm one of your sheep."

"You're only pretending to be a sheep," said the shepherd. "I'm no fool. I know you're really a wolf."

"How do you know?" asked the wolf. "I look like a sheep."

"You say you are a sheep," said the shepherd, "but you act like a wolf."

The shepherd pulled a limb from a tree and beat the wolf with it. The wolf leaped the fence and climbed a nearby hill. He never went back to the sheep pen.

The challenge is wolves in sheep's clothing don't look like wolves. They are disguised to look like sheep—hardworking employees, faithful tithers, and otherwise loyal companions. Jesus said you will know the wolves in sheep's clothing by their fruit (see Matt. 7:16). Fruit takes time to mature, so we must be both patient and discerning. We must understand, like the shepherd in the story, the behavior of the wolf.

SAVAGE WOLVES WILL COME

I function as a pastor at Awakening House of Prayer in Ft. Lauderdale. As such, I am a shepherd of sorts, although an apostolic-prophetic one. In other words, pastor is not my fivefold office, but I have the heart of a shepherd. I've learned the hard way—and more than once—that everyone who comes in looking like sheep is not a sheep. Some people come into the church crying about the wounds they sustained in the last church, but they are really wolves in disguise who are just waiting for an opportunity to devour you and anyone else they can before they leave or get exposed.

Paul wrote these sobering words to the leaders of the church in Ephesus:

Therefore take heed to yourselves and to all the flock, among which the Holy Spirit has made you overseers, to shepherd the church of God which He purchased with His own blood. For I know this, that after my departure savage wolves will come in among you, not sparing the flock. Also from among yourselves men will rise up, speaking perverse things, to draw away the disciples after themselves. Therefore watch, and remember that for three years I did not cease to warn everyone night and day with tears (Acts 20:28-31).

My opening words bear repeating: wolves are not just within the four walls of the church—wolves are everywhere. Whether you are leader of a church, a leader of a business, a leader of your home, or a leader in any capacity, you are serving as a shepherd. And one of the shepherd's jobs is to protect the sheep from the wolves. That means you have to watch and pray like David did in the fields. David delivered the sheep from the mouth of the lion, and you will have to do the same because the enemy is roaming about like a roaring lion seeking someone to devour.

Unfortunately, some of the wolves are so charismatic that if you don't discern them before they deceive the sheep, it's almost impossible to deliver the sheep from the wolf's mouth. They become loyal to the wolf. Wolves have a way of turning the sheep against the pastor, tapping into the sheep's insecurities or unmet needs or even aspirations.

Essentially, Absalom was a wolf in David's kingdom. David, who delivered the sheep from the mouth of the lion and the bear, failed to keep watch over Israel while his wolf son was turning large numbers of his followers against him. Just as Absalom split Israel, church splits are usually the work of the wolf in sheep's clothing.

One of Aesop's fables offers:

> A wolf hung about near a flock of sheep for a long time, but made no attempt to molest them. The shepherd at first kept a sharp eye on him, for he naturally thought he meant mischief. But as time went by, and the wolf showed no inclination to meddle with the flock, he began to look upon him more as a protector than as an enemy; and when one day some errand took him to the city, he felt no uneasiness at leaving the wolf with the sheep. But as soon as his back was turned, the wolf attacked them and killed the greater number. When the shepherd returned and saw the havoc he had wrought, he cried, "It serves me right for trusting my flock to a wolf."

Remember, leader, you too are ultimately a sheep. You are part of Christ's flock. Jesus said, "Listen carefully: I am sending you out like sheep among wolves; so be wise as serpents, and innocent as doves [have no self-serving agenda]" (Matt. 10:16 AMP). Just as the serpent was more crafty than any beast of the field in Adam's day, the wolf is subtle, sly, and slick, and if you are not vigilant you will see him carry off your sheep in his mouth. Keep watch over the flock. Feed them with truth that renews their mind. Pray for discernment.

HOW WE MISS THE WOLVES

If you are a shepherd, you probably failed to discern the wolf in your midst at least once over the years. Discernment is a gift of the spirit, but we can cultivate natural discernment as well—and we need to because wolves are multiplying rapidly.

A wolf came into our church under the guise of a son. He and his wife were very honoring toward me in the pulpit but behind my back were wooing people to do volunteer work in their ministry. They had people translating materials into other languages, editing books, and various other tasks. I had no idea. He was calling some of them his own sons and daughters and prophesying over their lives in private phone calls. My sheep thought he told me about it.

He fooled them, and me, for about two months. Then the Lord exposed it suddenly. When I confronted it, everyone felt duped and some of the younger ones were hurt. They thought he had their best interests at heart. Even others outside the ministry reported back to me that he was trying to get them to disconnect from me and serve his ministry. It ran deep and it took months to clean up. How did I miss it? I always had a little feeling that something was not right. I didn't want to act too quickly. It turned out I did not act quickly enough to discern what the Holy Spirit was trying to show me.

Discernment is "the quality of being able to grasp and comprehend what is obscure," also "an act of perceiving or discerning something," according to *Merriam-Webster*. Discerning means "able to see and understand people, things, or situations clearly and intelligently." Solomon didn't actually pray for wisdom. He prayed for discernment.

You have to become expert at knowing people by the spirit—and testing the spirits in which they are operating. Paul warned, "Check out everything, and keep only what's good. Throw out anything tainted with evil" (1 Thess. 5:21 MSG).

Discernment is the manifestation of biblical thinking rather than worldly thinking. That's why you have to renew your mind. Discernment is a spiritual discipline. It's a heart posture that listens to the Lord rather than taking everything at face value. Charles Spurgeon, a 19th century pastor they called the "Prince of Preachers," said this: "Discernment is not a matter of simply telling the difference between right and wrong; rather it is telling the difference between right and almost right."

We miss the wolf in sheep's clothing in many ways. We miss it because we're not paying attention. We miss it because we want to believe the best. We miss it because we look at the outward appearance rather than discerning the spirit behind the actions. We miss it because we look at charisma over character, or because someone is tremendously gifted. We miss it because we're distracted. We miss it because we ignore the Holy Spirit's warning—that check in our spirit that something is not right. We miss it because we don't listen to the warnings of others. Ask the Lord to help you not to miss it.

DISCERNING THE BIG BAD WOLF

Not all wolves are false prophets, but every wolf I've seen operates in prophetic witchcraft. They operate in high levels of deception, and they've honed their craft to the point that even the most discerning shepherds have to do a double or triple take to see through the sheepskin that hides their true identity. It's your job to at least try to catch them. If you are a shepherd appointed by God, you need to take this responsibility as seriously as He does. Ezekiel 34:7-10 reads:

> Therefore, you shepherds, hear the word of the Lord: "As I live," says the Lord God, "surely because My flock became a prey, and My flock became food for every beast of the field, because there was no shepherd, nor did My shepherds search

*for My flock, but the shepherds fed themselves and did not feed
My flock"—therefore, O shepherds, hear the word of the Lord!
Thus says the Lord God: "Behold, I am against the shepherds,
and I will require My flock at their hand; I will cause them to
cease feeding the sheep, and the shepherds shall feed themselves
no more; for I will deliver My flock from their mouths, that
they may no longer be food for them."*

I'm quite sure you don't fit this description in Ezekiel, but some pastors do. And their sheep are prey to wolves. While we can't wolf-proof our organizations entirely, we can be so vigilant that the wolves will look for another flock to devour just as a burglar goes for the easy-target houses where windows are open and doors are unlocked.

Wolves have keen senses, and they know when you are catching on to them. They are slick doubt-casters with the ability to deny undeniable evidence about their devouring motives. The key to protecting the sheep from the wolf and his prophetic witchcraft is to discern this inconspicuous predator before he strikes. Here are some behaviors and characteristics of wolves in sheep's clothing that will help you discern.

Wolves Are Predators Poised to Devour

While sheep are docile, wolves are predatory. Wolves will travel far and wide to catch and find their prey, often moving in on unsuspecting kills at night. Wolves take on the predatory nature of satan, who comes to steal, kill, and destroy (see John 10:10). In an article titled "Stalked by Satan," Mike Ford writes:

> The great deceiver, more often than not, works under
> cover of darkness. As a skilled and experienced hunter, he
> patiently stalks his prey, invisible to them (invisible is about

as camouflaged as one can get!). His night vision is acute, his senses much sharper than ours. He sees us when we do not even know he is there! Even now—he's stalking us.[1]

Predators count on Christians walking in blind love and quick trust, but just because it walks like a sheep and talks like a sheep doesn't mean it's a sheep. Often when a sheep spots the wolf and cries out, the other sheep persecute the discerning sheep and ignore the warning because they are already under the wolf's spell. That's where shepherds come in. Shepherds have to be vigilant against the preying wolf.

Wolves Target the Most Vulnerable

Wolves often target lone sheep—or vulnerable sheep. Remember the grandma in *Little Red Riding Hood*? She was elderly and sickly when the Big Bad Wolf devoured her. New or naïve believers are easy prey for the wolf's prophetic witchcraft.

Hurt and wounded believers are just as susceptible because the prophetic witchcraft speaks fabricated encouragement to their skewed souls. Offended sheep, too, are in danger because they are prone to isolate themselves from those who truly care about their wellbeing. The wolf's prophetic witchcraft speaks into that offense and makes a mountain out of their molehill.

Wolves Are Masters in Disguise

Wolves are masterful in disguising their true identity. They don't just look like sheep. They look like whatever you need them to be in your life so you will open the door to their devouring agenda. Wolves in sheep's clothing are spiritual chameleons of sorts, transforming themselves into something acceptable to their victim just as satan transforms himself into an angel of light (see 2 Cor. 11:14). Wolves study you to determine the greatest desires of your heart, then prophesy into those desires.

Wolves Put on Decorative Aprons

Wolves look for a quick place of service in any organization. They come willing to serve in the areas where you need it the most and appear to be godsends—the perfect solution to the problem you've been praying about. Of course, they prefer to serve in a place of visibility where they can position themselves in a way that draws victims to them. In church, that may be the worship team or leading a small group. In the workplace, that may be in some administrative role that touches various aspects of the company. Wolves want to have their claws in everything.

Wolves Have a Different Vision

Wolves never buy into the vision of the house; rather, they have a different vision—and their vision did not come from the Lord. It's a self-serving vision and they use prophetic witchcraft to manipulate people to adopt their vision instead of yours. This is not a new problem. Jeremiah 23:16 reads, "Thus says the Lord of hosts: 'Do not listen to the words of the prophets who prophesy to you. They make you worthless; they speak a vision of their own heart, not from the mouth of the Lord.'"

Wolves Are Territorial

Once a wolf gains position, they are highly territorial. More than that, they work to extend their boundaries beyond the authority that's been delegated to them so they expand the pool of possible victims. Just as wolves in the natural can consume up to nine pounds of meat at once, wolves in the spirit are insatiable. They will use prophetic witchcraft to get a seat at your table, and then devour you.

Wolves Have Strong Discernment

In the natural, wolves rely on their keen senses of hearing and smell—corresponding to discernment—to determine vulnerable prey. Wolves listen to disgruntled people's complaints and prophesy solutions. They listen to the sheep's discouraged hearts and prophesy encouragement. They listen to their frustrations and prophesy breakthrough. Based on the sheep's reaction to the bait, the wolf decides whether to go in for the kill.

Wolves Won't Accept Discipline

You may have heard that a wolf is in the canine family. The difference between a wolf and a dog is a dog can be corrected but a wolf rejects all discipline. When you confront a wolf in sheep's clothing, they will deny it. They will be defensive. They may get angry. They may point the finger back to you and blame you for the situation. If they are savvier, they will offer false repentance.

Wolves Manifest Bad Fruit

Ultimately, it takes fruit time to manifest. But if you are familiar with the fruit of the Spirit it won't take all that long to see that the wolf bears bad fruit. Galatians 5:22-23 outlines the fruit of the Spirit, "But the fruit of the Spirit is love, joy, peace, longsuffering, kindness, goodness, faithfulness, gentleness, self-control. Against such there is no law." Wolves may appear super spiritual, but their fruit is fake.

Wolves Work to Devour the Shepherd

If the shepherd catches on to the covert operations of wolves in sheep's clothing, the wolf turns to destroy the shepherd. They understand the words in Zechariah 13:7, "Strike the Shepherd, and the sheep will be scattered." The wolves will make false accusations against the shepherd to discredit them in the eyes of the sheep and win their hearts.

Wolves Are Cowardly

Wolves act big and bad but when you confront them and stand your ground, they will eventually flee. They will eventually fade out of the picture. And you can rebuild—but first you have to expose. As Paul wrote, "And have no fellowship with the unfruitful works of darkness, but rather expose them" (Eph. 5:11). If you don't expose them, you are letting them fellowship with your sheep.

PROTECTING THE FLOCK

Look again at these words Paul wrote to the leaders of the church in Ephesus:

> *Therefore take heed to yourselves and to all the flock, among which the Holy Spirit has made you overseers, to shepherd the church of God which He purchased with His own blood. For I know this, that after my departure savage wolves will come in among you, not sparing the flock. Also from among yourselves men will rise up, speaking perverse things, to draw away the disciples after themselves. Therefore watch, and remember that for three years I did not cease to warn everyone night and day with tears* (Acts 20:28-31).

The sheepdog—a dog the shepherd uses to help tend, drive, or guard the sheep—protects the flock. How do we do that? It's best to guard against the wolf before he gets entrenched in the sheepfold. As the leader, that means you need to be alert. Or, as Paul puts it in Acts 20:31, "watch."

The Greek word for *watch* in Acts 20:31 is *gregoreuo*. According to *The KJV New Testament Greek Lexicon*, it means "watch," but metaphorically the lexicon defines it with more drama: "give strict attention to, be cautious, active; to take heed lest through remission and indolence some destructive calamity suddenly overtake one." Watching for wolves is a serious matter. You can learn more about watching in my book *The Making of a Watchman*.

You'll need help watching. The task is too big for any one leader. Everyone should be watchful, vigilant, against the incoming wolf. Of course, there's a difference between going on a wolf watch and going on a witch hunt. Discernment disguised as suspicion can damage the flock, too. The key is to build a culture of true discernment and transparency where the sheep feel free to cry wolf. Then we can avoid a lot of the devouring.

EVICTING THE WOLF

Hireling shepherds—shepherds who don't care about the flock—won't bother with the wolf. Jesus put it this way:

> *I am the good shepherd. The good shepherd gives His life for the sheep. But a hireling, he who is not the shepherd, one who does not own the sheep, sees the wolf coming and leaves the sheep and flees; and the wolf catches the sheep and scatters them. The hireling flees because he is a hireling and does not care about the sheep* (John 10:11-13).

The bottom line is if you don't truly care about the sheep, you shouldn't be a shepherd. But I know if you are reading this you do care about the sheep. And that means you have to warn the congregation of the danger, and risk them not believing you. It also means you have to confront the wolf in the pasture.

John Calvin, a French lawyer, theologian, and reformer in the second generation of the Protestant Movement, wrote these words in *The Bondage and Liberation of the Will*:

> A faithful dog barks at the first sound of a thief and risks his own life to protect his master's life and his family—shall the church be plundered by the thieving of the ungodly, shall God's majesty be stamped under foot, shall Christ be robbed of his own kingdom, while we watch and say nothing?[2]

The bark is the warning. But after the warning is validated, the wolf has to be confronted. Moses confronted Pharaoh to deliver the flock. Elijah confronted the false prophets at Mt. Carmel to turn the flock's heart back to the Lord. Jesus taught us how to confront people who are walking in sin in Matthew 18:15-17:

> *Moreover if your brother sins against you, go and tell him his fault between you and him alone. If he hears you, you have gained your brother. But if he will not hear, take with you one or two more, that "by the mouth of two or three witnesses every word may be established." And if he refuses to hear them, tell it to the church. But if he refuses even to hear the church, let him be to you like a heathen and a tax collector.*

This is the biblical way to handle conflict. Usually, the wolf will not repent—or if they do you have to watch out for false repentance. Usually, the wolf will deny the allegations, feign hurt and offense, and leave. While we'd like to see the wolf repent, it's usually better for the wolf to leave the flock. Paul the apostle put it this way:

> For there are many insubordinate, both idle talkers and deceivers, especially those of the circumcision, whose mouths must be stopped, who subvert whole households, teaching things which they ought not, for the sake of dishonest gain. One of them, a prophet of their own, said, 'Cretans are always liars, evil beasts, lazy gluttons.' This testimony is true. Therefore rebuke them sharply, that they may be sound in the faith (Titus 1:10-13).

Yes, rebuke them sharply.

In closing, consider one of Aesop's fables:

> A tricky old wolf once entered a farm, and seeing oats growing, he put on his charm, so, calmly pretending that he meant no harm, he spoke to a horse in his stall. "Sir Horse, I do hope you are comfortably fed, but in case you are hungry and famished instead, there are oats by the ton in one field," he said, "and I ate none so you'd have all."
>
> Now the horse knew quite well that the wolf hated oats and cared nothing for horses—or cattle or goats, and in fact was well known for attacking their throats, so he couldn't resist ridicule: "Sir Wolf," he said, "don't think me over-suspicious were I to suspect there was something

malicious in your lying claim you find oats delicious. *Begone!* Do you think me a fool?"

Don't be foolish. Boldly evict the wolf. Just as the wolf has to stand before Jesus one day, so does the shepherd. Your responsibility is to the flock, not the wolf.

NOTES

1. Mike Ford, "Stalked By Satan," *Forerunner,* "Ready Answer," September, 1993, https://pdf.cgg.org/Stalked-by-Satan-631.pdf.

2. John Calvin, *The Bondage and Liberation of the Will* (Grand Rapids, MI: Baker Books, 1996), 19.

ABOUT
JENNIFER LECLAIRE

Jennifer LeClaire is senior leader of Awakening House of Prayer in Fort Lauderdale, Florida, founder of the Ignite Network, and founder of the Awakening Prayer Hubs prayer movement. Jennifer formerly served as the first-ever female editor of *Charisma* magazine and is a prolific author of over 50 books. You can find Jennifer online or shoot her an email at info@jenniferleclaire.org.

Notes